MEETING WITH
OUR LADY OF MEDJUGORJE

Finbar O'Leary

Meeting with
Our Lady of Medjugorje

❦ ❦ ❦

With Prayer Group Messages
from Ivan, Marijana, Marija, Jelena, & Fr Slavko

the columba press

First published in 2014 by
the columba press
55A Spruce Avenue, Stillorgan Industrial Park,
Blackrock, Co. Dublin

Cover by Red Rattle Design
Origination by The Columba Press
Printed by Bell & Bain Ltd

ISBN 978 1 78218 141 5

www.columba.ie

I accept that the final authority regarding the Apparitions at Medjugorje rests with the Holy See of Rome, to whose judgement I willingly submit.

Finbar O'Leary

Contents

Pray and fast!
Know that I love you.
I hold all of you on my knees.

Introduction

I Want A Prayer Group Here
At the end of March 1983, Our Lady at Medjugorje announced through a ten-year-old girl that She wished a prayer group to be formed. This group was to be guided by Our Lady through that child, little Jelena. The words of Our Lady to Jelena were:

> I want a prayer group here. I will lead the group and give rules of sanctification to it. Through these rules all others in the world can consecrate themselves. I will give you one month to choose this group, but tell them the conditions I lay down.
>
> First of all, they have to renounce every-thing, putting themselves totally at God's disposition. Renounce all fear because if they are abandoned to God there is no place for fear. All difficulties they encounter will be for their spiritual growth and for the Glory of God.
>
> I prefer young people because married people have commitments and the obligation to work. But everyone who wants to participate in this programme can, at least, follow it in part. I will lead this group.

An extraordinary statement one might think. But then, the whole spiritual phenomena unfolding in Medjugorje has been extraordinary. And yet, as with Medjugorje itself, there is a simplistic beauty in this picture of a mother and child, a mother's call to all her children to be sanctified.

To understand the context of this request from Our Blessed Mother, let us take a brief look at the beginning of the Medjugorje event.

Rome, May 1981
While in Rome for a prayer conference during May 1981, the renowned Sr Briege McKenna, who has experienced more of the extraordinary workings of Jesus and the Holy Spirit than most Christians could ever imagine, was approached by Fr Tomislav Vlasic OFM from Bosnia-Herzegovina, in what is now the former Yugoslavia, asking if she would pray over him. During the prayers she received one of the images from Our Lord she so often gets when praying over people. She saw a large white church with twin steeples; from the celebrant's chair in the sanctuary, streams of living water flowed down past the altar with thousands of people coming to drink this water. Fr Tomislav was greatly uplifted by this holy image. His country was going through a difficult time. The communist government was less than sympathetic towards the Church.

Our Lady Appears
Less than a month later, in June 1981, the feast of St John the Baptist, four girls and two boys, were walking between two villages in Bosnia-Herzegovina when suddenly they saw on the hillside a phenomena which they recognised as Our Lady (The 'Gospa'). They were frightened and ran

away. The following day they were moved in their hearts to go there again to pray. After praying awhile, they saw again Our Lady on the mountainside. Our Lady beckoned them to Her with Her hand as though She wanted to embrace them and gather them together. Then they started to run with such speed that nobody could keep up with them. They said afterwards that they felt as if they were being carried by someone. When they arrived up the mountain they saw a beautiful girl of 18–20 years of age. One of the seers sprinkled this girl, this phenomenon, saying: 'I sprinkle you with holy water; if you are from Satan go away; if you are from God stay with us.'

She smiled and said:

I am the Blessed Virgin Mary.

Our Lady's Message

Our Lady has given Her main message, that is *mir*, which means peace. Several times Our Lady has told the visionaries that the world lives in great tension and that the world cannot be saved if it continues like this. The world has to find peace to be saved, but it will not find peace without God. It will only find peace in God, therefore Our Lady asks for conversions. In the early days when Our Lady pronounced the message of peace, it was written in the sky – *mir*, the Croatian word for peace. Many thousands of people saw it. I have already said that Our Lady asks for conversions in order to attain peace with God. This call for conversion is urgent. A message was given to one of the visionaries with the following words:

Tell all my sons and daughters, tell all the world as soon as possible that I desire their conversion. The only word I tell the world is, convert and do not delay. I will ask my Son not to punish the world but that the world be saved. You do not, and cannot, know what God will send to the world. Convert, renounce everything, be ready for everything, because all this is part of the conversion.

Our Lady repeated Her call to conversion by saying:

Tell the world not to wait, it needs to convert. When God comes He will not be joking; I tell you that you must take my messages seriously.

Our Lady calls for prayer and fasting:

If you are not able to fast on water and bread, you can give up various things. It would be very good to give up television since after watching the programmes you are distracted and unable to pray. You can renounce alcohol, cigarettes and other pleasures. You know yourselves what you must do.

Our Lady has called us to take up once more the practice of monthly confession, as She has asked us to do at Fatima. Our Lady said:

If Christians went to confession every month, reconciling themselves with God and their neighbours, whole Christian communities would soon be spiritually healed.

Our Lady wants peace and is calling us to peace, conversion, prayer, fasting and to a sacramental life. These messages repeat themselves over and over.

From the first day, Our Lady has continued to appear daily. The six visionaries are Ivanka, Mirjana, Ivan, Vicka, Marija and Jakov. The apparitions of which they speak are the three-dimensional type; that is, they see Our Lady as a real person; She comes in Her risen body. They talk to Her, they can touch Her, they pray together. They relate to Her as they would to a normal person. From the moment when Our Lady appears they do not see anything else in front of them, nor do they react at all. She introduced herself to the visionaries with a specific name:

> I am the Blessed Virgin Mary and wish to be known here as Queen of Peace.

Visionaries and Secrets

Three of the visionaries have received nine secrets each and continue to see Our Lady every day, no matter where, or what part of the world they happen to be. The other three visionaries, Ivanka, Mirjana and Jakov, received ten secrets and now see Our Lady only on special occasions.

Mirjana is the visionary chosen to announce the two admonitory signs, that is to say, the first and second secrets, which will precede the visible, permanent and indestructible sign (third secret). On the evening of her final daily apparition Mirjana said that Our Lady told her:

> Now you have to turn to God through faith like everyone else. I will appear to you on your birthday and when you encounter difficulties in life.

All the visionaries say that the secrets, in substance, affect the whole world. There are private secrets for some of them, concerning their future, but the important secrets relate to the whole world. One of the secrets has been revealed by the visionaries. They say that Our Lady has promised to leave a visible sign on the hill where the first apparitions occurred:

> This sign will be given for atheists. You faithful already have signs and you have to become the sign for the atheists.

Following this visible sign there will be many miracles and healings. All the visionaries say that they have seen this sign in the apparitions, they know the date when the sign will come; but they say that before the sign comes there will be a warning or admonishment to the world. Our Lady says this about the sign:

> You faithful must not wait for the sign before you convert; convert soon, this time is a time of grace for you. You can never thank God enough for this grace, which He has given you. The time is for deepening your faith and for your conversion. When the sign comes it will be too late for many.

Powerful messages were given in the autumn of 1983. Through Jakov, Our Lady said:

> I have already said several times that peace in the world is in danger; have brotherly love for each other, increase your prayers and fasting so that you may be saved.

Jakov said that everyone must be told this. Then, on 30 November 1983, Our Lady told Marija to tell the priest:

You must advise the Bishop and the Pope at once of the urgency and great importance of this message for the whole of humanity.

Prayer, Penance and Fasting

From the start, Our Lady emphasised that conversion can happen only through prayers and fasting. She first called the people to pray daily the Our Father, Hail Mary and Glory Be at least seven times each, and to recite the Creed; also to fast on Fridays on bread and water. Our Lady said:

You have forgotten that with prayer and fasting you can even avert wars: you can even suspend natural laws. Nobody is exempt from fasting. Fasting cannot be substituted by giving alms, only the sick can substitute it by almsgiving and the sacraments. But you all have to pray, fast and give alms. Fasting is avoiding sin. But one must also fast with the body. The fasting you do by eating fish instead of meat is not fasting. Real fasting is eating only bread and water.

Inner Locution

In the course of this book we will refer to the visionaries, particularly Ivan and Marija, but in the main, concern ourselves with the two young girls, close friends and distant cousins Jelena Vasilj and Marijana Vasilj, both of whom received the gift of inner locution: deeply mystical experiences whereby Jesus and Our Lady communicate messages and images interiorly. They can only converse or experience on spiritual matters. A somewhat similar phenomena to that experienced by Fr Gobbi and Sr Briege McKenna.

Fr Slavko Barbaric

Fr Slavko Barbaric OFM, a doctor of social psychology who went to Medjugorje to investigate the event, published a methodical analysis of the six visionaries in 1982 and undertook a further study of the two locutionaries the following year. In the fullness of time Fr Slavko became spiritual director to the visionaries and highly respected internationally for his warm and deeply spiritual reflections on the continued presence of Our Lady (The 'Gospa'), Her messages, and their developing fruits throughout the Church and the world.

Fr Tomislav Vlasic

Fr Tomislav Vlasic OFM, who we shall quote extensively, though prominent in the Medjugorje story, is perhaps not widely recognised, as a result of his committed involvement with Our Lady's prayer group since early 1983 and Our Lady's request that this should be a closed group and develop free from the intrusion of public interruption.

The Commission

On 9 January 1987, Cardinal Franjo Kuraric announced the formation of the new commission to examine events at Medjugorje as requested from Rome by Cardinal Ratzinger (later Pope Benedict XVI), who had responsibility for the propagation of the faith. In a statement Cardinal Ratzinger explained that Medjugorje would be examined on two levels: the facts, that is the visionaries themselves; and the fruits of the event.

Living Water

Of all the streams of living water flowing from Medjugorje since that faithful day in June 1981, surely no stream of grace is more full of the fruits than the stream from the Gospa's prayer group, which is nothing less than Mary's very own school of prayer, where all of us are invited to participate, to pray from the heart, to grow in the Holy Spirit and form prayer groups in every family and every parish.

The Century of Satan

If we look at what Our Lady is saying through the visionaries during this period we shall perhaps have a greater understanding of Our Lady's desire to guide a prayer group (school of prayer) from which others in time may learn and follow.

Mirjana had a particular vision on 14 April 1982; while she was waiting for Our Lady to appear, Satan arrived disguised as Our Lady. She explains:

> He was ugly, horribly ugly. You cannot even imagine how ugly, he almost killed me with his gaze, I almost fainted. He told me, 'You must leave God and Our Lady because they will make you suffer, come with me and I will make you happy in love and life!' My heart echoed: No, No, No! Then Satan went away and Our Lady came and said to me: 'I am sorry for this, but you must know that Satan exists and has asked God to allow him to test the Church for a certain period with the intention of destroying Her. God allowed him to have one century, saying: "You will not destroy Her." This century in which we are living is under Satan's

power. When the secrets I have confided to you come about, his power will be destroyed. Satan has become aggressive because he is losing his power. He is breaking up marriages, causing quarrels amongst priests, obsessing people, even killing them. Therefore, protect yourselves by prayer, fasting and, above all, community prayer. Renew the use of holy water, wear blessed and holy objects and put them in your houses.'

This vision is similar to that which Pope Leo XIII had a century ago when he saw the Church attacked by demons in an apocalyptic vision. Afterwards, he introduced the prayer to St Michael the Archangel to be recited by the priest after Mass and was said until the second Vatican Council.

Jelena Vasilj
Locutionary

Jelena Vasilj through her formative years has grown from being a lovable, modest child, to the beautiful demure lady she is today. Always so unpretentious, even disarming in her modesty and gentleness, Jelena through her love for Jesus and Mary, and her openness to the workings of the Holy Spirit exudes an extraordinary sense of peace and confidence upon all who come within her sphere through her words. Her beautiful eyes seem to penetrate your very soul when speaking with her. When she speaks on matters of faith or leads you in prayer, you sense the depth, the very essence of her subjectiveness to the will of God.

Born on 14 May 1972, Jelena was just ten years of age when the 'Gospa' first appeared to the six young visionaries. She and her little friend Marijana, responding to Our Lady's call, would spend much of their free time praying together instead of playing with their friends.

Jelena was granted the gift of inner locution (hearing Our Lady's voice and later that of Jesus) on 15 December 1982. Just two weeks later, on 29 December, she was granted a second gift, that of seeing Our Lady within her heart, later she would also see Jesus. Jelena blossomed in prayer over the next three months, always guided by Our Lady.

Our Lady told Jelena that this gift of inner locution would also be granted to

na and the little five-year-old Anita if they prayed more. They saw Our Lady for the first time on Good Friday 1983. Again through Jelena, Our Lady said that if both the girls continued with prayer and fasting they would receive the gift of *Locuto Interno* (hearing Her voice). Marijana persevered and on 5 August 1983 heard the voice of Our Lady for the first time.

This phenomenon is, at the same time, divergent from and convergent with the other phenomenon of the six visionaries. That is to say that the separate accounts of everything that Our Lady has told the six visionaries confirm what She is saying to Jelena. Our Lady told Jelena at the beginning:

> I do not intend to reveal the secrets through you, but rather to guide you on the path to consecration to God.

In this young girl we can in fact see very strong spiritual dynamics with many spiritual experiences.

A Family at Prayer

Like almost all families in Medjugorje at that time, Jelena's family responded to Our Lady's call with great humility and openness of heart. Gargo Vasilj, Jelena's father, tells us that

> since the apparitions, much has changed in the way we live. Indeed, we prayed before. However, now we pray much more and, more importantly, I see more clearly that I'm a sinner and that I need to pray even more. God has given me the grace to recognise this. This is the

essence of everything, and it's most important because God will then allow me to convert. It's essential that Jesus be glorified. It's not important that it's sometimes hard for us to do. For example, we see how different everything is now and how it has influenced our family life.

At the beginning of Our Lady's apparitions, everything was much quieter here. Now the pilgrims often come and visit us. I'm sure that Jesus wants us to form a community with the pilgrims. That means the pilgrims should not go home empty-handed, but should take something with them. God expects us to fulfil our mission, and it's perfectly clear that He has a plan for us. So we, who have been witnessing the events, have received a great grace, but also a big responsibility.

Next to the mission of forming a community with the pilgrims who come to us, I feel that Jesus expects harmony in the family. He wants all of us in the family to live in communion: parents, grandparents and children, so that three generations live together. This can often be difficult, but we have to take it upon ourselves even if we suffer by it. Jesus has shown us with His passion that suffering has its own meaning. And the goal is significant: it is unity, community, a healthy family, a healthy core. If we are a healthy family, then we can be useful to others. We have to pray about it and ask for it. In my family we surrender all our difficulties to Jesus, and pray for this; and I believe that He, in His goodness, will always help us.

We've been praying in this manner for quite a bit, but I believe that we still don't pray enough and that we should pray much more. In our family it goes like this: First, we read a section from the Bible, then we pray the rosary and the litanies, we sing a song to the Holy Spirit, and pray a few more prayers. At noon, we pray the Angelus and, in the evening, we go to Mass. Regretfully, because of the events and the many visitors, we have less time to teach our children even though we see more clearly how they should be raised.

Regarding Jelena, I think that as her father I have a significant role. Now, I definitely see that every person has his or her given roles. When I see, for example, how our priests preach here, I think that all priests in the world should preach that way. Then there would be more good in the world, Jesus would be more glorified; and that would be good for all of us.

This is a short, simple statement of fact. Short in words but so responsive in action to the call of Our Blessed Mother to 'pray, pray, pray'. There is nothing complicated in what Mary is asking from us, nothing we can not understand, just simply pray. Prayer should be something simple, like a talk with friends. Only when we receive God in the simplicity of our heart will our prayer be authentic. Simplicity in a prayer is very important. It is also important that we be humble before Our God, make ourselves small. Prayer can still have its diversity, for example through reading Holy Scripture. It is only the simplicity in us that will allow the Holy Spirit to speak to us and inspire us, as the Holy Spirit is quite clearly inspiring Gargo Vasilj.

The Prayer Group

At the end of March 1983 Our Lady told Jelena of Her desire to have a prayer group formed:

> I desire a prayer group here. I will lead the group and give rules for sanctification to it. Through these rules all others in the world can consecrate themselves.

The parishioners were given one month to decide whether to be part of this group or not. Through Jelena Our Lady gave rules for the group:

One: First of all they have to renounce everything, putting themselves totally in God's hands; renounce all fear because if they are abandoned to God there is no place for fear. All difficulties they encounter will be for their spiritual growth and for the glory of God.

It was a difficult decision for the parishioners to make, and so Our Lady gave some advice:

Two: I prefer young people because married people have family commitments and obligations to work. But everyone who wants to participate in this programme can, at least follow it in part. I will lead this group.

Clearly the invitation was for all, even if only partial participation was possible. However, Our Lady did state a preference:

Three: Preferably bring together those who belong to the meditation prayer group.

Four: Abandon yourselves to God without restrictions.

Five: Definitely eliminate all anguish. Whoever abandons himself to God does not have room in His heart for anguish. Difficulties will persist, but they will serve for spiritual growth and for the glory of God.

Six: Love your enemies. Banish hatred from your heart; bitterness, preconceived judgements. Pray for your enemies and call the divine blessing over them.

Seven: Fast twice a week on bread and water.

Eight: Join the group at least once a week.

Nine: Devote at least three hours to prayers daily, at least half an hour in the morning and half an hour in the evening. Holy Mass and the prayers of the rosary (fifteen decades) are included in this time of prayer. Set aside moments of prayer in the course of the day and each time that circumstances permit it, receive Holy Communion. Pray with great meditation. Do not look at your watch all the time, but allow yourself to be led by the grace of God. Do not concern yourselves too much with the things of this world, but entrust everything in prayer to Our Heavenly Father. If one is very preoccupied, he will not be able to pray well because internal serenity is lacking.

Those who attend school or go to work must pray half an hour in the morning and in the evening, and if possible, participate in the Eucharist (Mass). It is necessary to extend the spirit of prayer to daily work, that is to say, to accompany work with prayers.

Ten: Pray very much for the Bishops and for those who hold positions in the Church. No less than half of their prayers and sacrifices must be devoted to this intention.

A four-year commitment to the group was requested (on 20 October 1983):

Eleven: This is not the time for you to choose your vocation. The important thing is to start praying straight away. Afterwards you will make the right choice.

Twelve: The Blessed Virgin said, although She would guide the group through Jelena, that 'the group should have a priest'. Fr Tomislav has acted as spiritual director for the group from its beginning.

Through Jelena, Our Lady sent a message to the world on 25 April 1983:

Tell all my sons and daughters that my heart is burning for them. I ask only for conversion, only conversion.

Fr Tomislav then asked Our Lady through Jelena if he should tell this to the Pope and Our Lady replied:

> To all as quickly as possible. The word I tell the world is 'be converted'. I will pray to my Son not to punish the world, but you must be converted. You do not know, you will not know and cannot know what God will send the world; you must be converted. Renounce everything and be ready for everything. That is all I wish to tell the world: be converted.

This message was given in an atmosphere of a thousand questions from the clergy, the Bishop and priests who were saying: who knows if She has appeared, how She has appeared, why She has appeared at Medjugorje, why not in another parish; why, why, why? Then Our Lady simply said:

> The word I want to tell the world is: be converted.

Sr Janja

Sr Janja, a Franciscan sister teaching in Medjugorje, tells us:

The invitation to join the prayer group was announced in the church. Some fifty-nine young people, as well as four older women, took part. So what has become known as 'Our Lady's' or the 'main' prayer group came into being. The average age was about twenty. Some of the young people had not yet finished secondary school. Others worked, mostly in the fields tending to the tobacco and grape vines. The group began with a one-month period of prayer and fasting during which each person made a decision whether or not to respond personally to this call from Mary, whether or not to make the four-year commitment.

Sr Janja with one of the children from 'Mother's Village'
(orphanage) in Medjugorje.

On the feast of the second anniversary of the apparitions at Medjugorje, the Queen of Peace commenced in earnest Her guidance of the group.

Sr Janja, herself a member of the group, tells us that one day through Jelena, Our Lady said:

> You are not able to fulfil your duties because you pray too little. ... When there are difficulties, I will ask you to fast and pray more. You have begun to pray for three hours, but why do you keep looking at your watches? You are too taken up with how you should do your work and get it finished. I want to tell you that you will never finish it that way. You must let the Spirit lead you in a deep way. Leave your

worries aside. Offer your time to God. You will be able to get everything done and you will even have time to spare.

Six weeks later Our Lady said:

Now listen carefully. You have decided to follow Jesus' way, to consecrate yourselves totally to Him. When someone tries to follow God unreservedly, Satan comes and attempts to steer him away from what he has begun. This is a time of testing. Satan will tell you, you are doing too much.

Be prudent because the devil tempts all those who have made a resolution to consecrate themselves to God, most particularly those people. He will suggest to them that they are praying too much, they are fasting too much, that they must be like other young people and go in search of pleasures. Have them not listen to him nor obey him. It is to the voice of the Blessed Virgin that they should pay attention. When they will be strengthened in their faith, the devil will no longer be able to seduce them.

It seems clear that the prayer group is a kind of four-year formation programme. Above all, it is a school of prayer. Mary has guided and taught the group through Jelena mostly, but as time went on also through Mirjana. The prophetic words that come to them through Mary stress the importance of prayer and teach how to pray. What matters is not so much the time spent or the number of prayers said, but to pray with love from the heart. Our Lady spent four weeks, during three meetings a week, lasting over two hours each, teaching the group how to meditate and pray the Our Father slowly. She also taught them a special way to pray the Jesus Rosary consisting of thirty-three Our Fathers, one for each year that Jesus lived among us.

The group do their best to love everyone that they have contact with, including any who oppose them in any way. They try to be helpful to all around them and they give no place to anger or resentment in their lives. They ask God every day to pour out His Holy Spirit on the whole world.

Our Lady told the group:

> I have come to tell the world that God is truth;
> He exists. True happiness and the fullness of life
> are in Him. I have come here as Queen of Peace
> to tell the world that peace is necessary for the
> salvation of the world. In God, one finds true
> joy from which true peace is derived.

Fr Svetozar Kraljevic OFM

Fr Svetozar Kraljevic OFM, who returned from America to minister in Medjugorje had this to say:

> The young locutionaries are becoming very important, especially the one named Jelena Vasilj. She experiences the voice and presence of Our Lady. Messages from Our Lady have been coming through her. Jelena is very intelligent, very pious and very open to spiritual things.

Like Fr Svet, Fr Rene Laurentin also believes Jelena is very important. Fr Tomislav Vlasic sees in Jelena the future. He believes that whatever is going to happen, is going to happen through her.

Fr Svet, as he is affectionately known to millions of pilgrims from all over the world.

Pray with Your Heart

It was through Jelena that Our Lady invited the people in the course of 1983 to learn to pray continuously and unceasingly (1 Thessalonians 5:17). The first invitation to learn the Prayer of the Heart was when She told Jelena:

> When I say 'Pray, pray, pray' I don't mean only increase the hours of prayer, but increase the desire to pray and to be in contact with God, to be in a continuously prayerful state of mind.

It was through Jelena that Our Lady has asked the people of the parish on the first day of Her school of prayer, to read a passage from St Matthew's Gospel 6:24–34. This passage was to be read on every subsequent Thursday as well. It relates how Jesus told the disciples to decide for God, to trust in God and to seek His Kingdom first. Clearly Our Lady is not telling us anything new about the spiritual life, but She is calling us back to the Gospel of Her Son, to live the life of God's children.

By reading the same passage of Scripture over and over again, the Word of God gradually establishes roots to our soul and heart, in the inner shrine of being, helping us to learn the 'unceasing prayer', the Prayer of the Heart, the ultimate form of prayer which transforms us into the likeness of Jesus Christ. Seeing Jesus in such deep prayer prompted the disciples to ask Him: 'Lord, teach us to pray' (Luke 11:1). In the course of the Thursday messages we hear time after time Our Lady's call to the Prayer of the Heart, that which St Paul calls the 'unceasing prayer'.

Our Lady, through Jelena, gave very practical guidance in learning the Prayer of the Heart (Holy Thursday, 19 April 1984) and because of its importance I quote the whole text:

> I will show you a spiritual secret; if you wish to be stronger than evil then you must create an active consciousness of God within yourself. To do this, you must give reasonable time for prayer each morning, read a text from Holy Scripture and implant the Divine Word in your heart. Then you must try to live it during the day, putting the Word of God into practice, especially in moments of trial. By the end of the day you will see the fruits of this – you will be stronger than the evil around you. You will become aware of God's working within yourself.

The early Desert Fathers practised this kind of Scripture reading. Following the teaching of St John Cassian and St Basil the Great, St Benedict in his Rule recommends this practice for those who wish 'to hasten to the perfection of religion' (ch. 73). In the Benedictine tradition – and, I am sure, in most religious communities – the regular reading of Holy Scripture is the source of deep prayer. It follows the classical stages: *lectio, meditatio, oratio*: contemplation, that is reading a text from Scripture, meditating on it, then praying about it, and finally contemplating on the central word or message of the text. Modern teachers of meditation call such a key work or sentence a mantra like the Jesus Prayer (Lord Jesus Christ, have mercy on me, a sinner.) repeating it not just in words on the lips but rather prayed by the whole person, in the depths of one's being, involving mind, body and spirit. That is what Prayer of the Heart is about. Prayer of the Heart means prayer not just of the emotions and affections, but of the whole person, including the body.

The biblical understanding of a person takes into account the mind–body–spirit reality of our being (1 Thessalonians 5:23).

> The heart, is not just simply the physical organ but the spiritual centre of man's being, man as made in the image of God, his deepest and truest self, or the inner shrine, to be entered only through sacrifice and death, in which the mystery of the union between the Divine and the human is consummated.
>
> *G.E.H. Palmer, Philip Sherrard, Kallistos Ware,*
> The Philokalia, *Vol. 1, p. 361.*

This is how the early Christian Fathers interpreted heart and the Prayer of the Heart, and a very important feature of the spirituality of the eastern churches.

The fact that Our Lady is using a young girl, a child, for conveying Her guidance to us to learn contemplative prayer, the Prayer of the Heart, the unceasing prayer, is an evidence in our time of the wonderful way God is communicating with His people, and is expressed beautifully in the prayer of Jesus:

> I bless you, Father, Lord of Heaven and earth, for hiding these things from the learned and the clever, and revealing them to little children.
>
> *Matthew 11:25*

*A rare photograph of the visionaries
in the early days of the apparitions.
(left to right) Ivan, Marija, Mirjana, Ivanka, Jakov, Vicka.*

Conversation with Jelena

One of the many uplifting experiences when on pilgrimage or retreat in Medjugorje is joining Jelena and Marijana for a prayer meeting.

While Medjugorje itself is a place of holiness, of tremendous peace and prayerfulness, when in their company one feels a certain serenity. A calmness seems to surround you, as though nothing else in the world is of any importance except to be here, to be still, quiet, to pray, to speak of the great love of Jesus, the love of Mary, Our Most Blessed Mother. Perhaps to sit in the warmth of glorious sunshine, and just for a little while, be like a student child with Jelena, in Mary's school of prayer.

FINBAR: Jelena, please tell us of your life at this time.

JELENA: My life with my family and friends, in school and in the community, hasn't changed much. Maybe now I live more consciously than before. My mother tells me that I prayed before, but I pray much more now, and God is closer to me.

When I was nine, ten, eleven years old, at an age when I could easily have strayed from God, Our Lady saved me from that. Recently Our

Lady cried, mostly on behalf of young people who have drifted so far away from God. She said that the devil is very powerful, and wants to destroy Her plans. She said that prayer is necessary. It touched my heart deeply and, at that same time, it made me happy that I see Her as my mother, Jesus as my friend and brother, and God as my father. They're so close to me; they help me and make me happy. I'm glad God doesn't want me to leave my friends. He wants me to tell them, and show them, by my prayer life, what God means to me.

FINBAR: Jelena, can you tell us about how you experienced the apparitions of the Mother of God?

JELENA: On 23 December 1982, I first heard the voice of the angel in school, during biology class. I heard this voice some days! It told me that I shall see the Mother of God. Since then I nearly always hear the voice. That was certainly a special time for us. I would say that this time not only brought a change in our lives but much more, it promoted our spiritual growth. I was ten years old then, and for me it was not only a change but the beginning of my growth in faith.

FINBAR: How did you grow in faith? How were you led by the Mother of God?

JELENA: She leads us, above all else, in prayer and She showed us in this way how we should live in the presence of Jesus in everyday life. She taught us that we should recognise His will in every situation and that we should bestir ourselves to recognise Jesus in every human being. Our Prayer should not be just a part of our duties but it should really be a meeting with Jesus, a tête-à-tête with God. The Mother of God said that we should say the rosary and that we should celebrate the Holy Mass. The most important thing is that we should do it with our hearts. The time I devote to prayer: in the morning, our family prayer. I usually go to Holy Mass in the evening. Three times per week we met after Mass to pray in the prayer group.

Regarding my personal prayer, I have no fixed time. I pray spontaneously whenever I have time which I wish to dedicate to God.

FINBAR: It is known that the Mother of God wanted a prayer group here in Medjugorje. She first expressed this call through you. Can you remember what this was like?

JELENA: I was eleven at the time. I remember that the Mother of God said to me that I should turn to a priest and that we should pray together.

FINBAR: Did you seek out the priest yourself or did the Mother of God?

JELENA: I don't know that I did. Fr Tomislav Vlasic had taken a special interest in the group.

FINBAR: Can you remember when Fr Tomislav had begun to guide your group?

JELENA: In 1983, a few months before New Year's Day [the first locution] the Mother of God had invited us to decide and then everything began – actually really only when the Mother of God had closed the circle of prayers [persons praying] in October of the same year.

FINBAR: What did the Mother of God want from the prayer group at the beginning?

JELENA: She wanted us to follow the way with Her, to devote three hours to daily prayer, to fast twice weekly and sometimes an extra day. She wanted that from all believers. Her particular request from our group was that every single member would commit himself for four years. She wanted us to follow Her for four years; that we would always be present at every prayer group meeting, because there would be no unity if we were only present at certain times. She demanded our presence/attendance so that we could grow together.

FINBAR: Did the Mother of God want you to dedicate yourselves completely to prayer?

JELENA: Yes, naturally She wants us to dedicate ourselves completely to prayer. It is important that we understand this 'complete dedication of oneself'. She hasn't actually demanded of us that we experience the presence of God in every moment of our daily lives. Prayer should be a help to us. Prayer should be a guiding light.

FINBAR: As a result of this prayer group, prayer groups have sprung up throughout the world. Can you say anything in particular for these prayer groups. The Mother of God has given messages for the prayer group through you?

JELENA: The only thing that seems to be important for the establishment and growth of a prayer group is that each individual works on himself; that he grows personally and consequently that he follows the path. If each one does not bear witness through his experience, then he causes obstacles to the development and growth of a prayer group. I think it is imperative that we all work together, that we become really active. Then there is that which depends on each group: the sort of prayer and the form of prayer.

FINBAR: The Mother of God asked for another prayer group, an inner circle. This circle is known as the 'small prayer group'. What in your opinion was the Mother of God's plan for this small prayer group?

JELENA: We, the [later] members of this small prayer group, were close – we were neighbours. So we had the opportunity to meet regularly, which we did. We prayed together and at one of these meetings the Mother of God asked us if we would like Her to help us in our growth in prayer. Naturally, we gladly accepted and so the small prayer group formed, which is part of the large prayer group.

FINBAR: Did the Mother of God not guide the small prayer group much more intensively especially in prayer? What was it like, the Mother of God's programme?

JELENA: We met very, very often; at the beginning even every day. The Mother of God gave us daily messages. She helped us so that we grew together even in prayer. She taught us a lot regarding spiritual life; She told us a lot. She explained a lot to us. It can be applied to the large prayer group. Today all members of the small group are also members of the big prayer group.

FINBAR: Can you describe a meeting of the small prayer group as directed by the Mother of God?

JELENA: The meetings were not all the same. We prayed in different ways. Very often we read the Holy Scripture – the reading of the Gospels – or we reflected on the messages which the Mother of God had given us. Afterwards we spoke about it and shared our thoughts and experiences. That was the main part of our meeting. Very often we said the rosary. Very often we prayed spontaneously and freely.

FINBAR: Did the Mother of God give messages for the family through you?

JELENA: Yes, very often, especially at that time when we prayed in the small prayer group. She stressed how important the family is for us. She said that there should be a place for prayer in every family – a prayer corner. She stressed that this should be a source of grace for the family.

FINBAR: What did She especially emphasise for families?

JELENA: The place of prayer, the common growth in prayer. In the first place She did not speak about completely concrete things, but She said that all messages are directed at everybody – to each member of the family. I also think, however, She did give special messages for the family at times but I cannot exactly remember.

FINBAR: What do you think about the future?

JELENA: Mine? It is still too early to talk of definite plans.

FINBAR: What do you think of the development here in Medjugorje?

JELENA: I certainly cannot close my eyes to the changes which have happened here in Medjugorje in recent years, but I think that God's plan for Medjugorje will be realised. I'm convinced that good will be victorious. I pray for that; I live for that; that is my hope.

FINBAR: Has the Mother of God said anything about Medjugorje recently? Are there any special messages for the priests or for the world?

JELENA: She gives messages, but I think they are of a broader nature, meant for all mankind as well as for the priests.

FINBAR: Are you sure it's Our Lady you see?

JELENA: Yes, quite sure. For when we imagine things it's just the power of our imagination at work. But when we meet Our Lady, She speaks words that are clearly audible and fill us with joy. Afterwards we are left with a feeling of deep peace, which confirms that it really was 'Gospa'.

FINBAR: When do you see Her?

JELENA: Usually in the evening after Mass, but sometimes during Holy Communion as well.

FINBAR: Can you explain what 'Prayer of the Heart' means?

JELENA: Many a time 'Gospa' has insisted on this. It means having a desire to pray; not praying out of habit simply because others are praying; praying out of a felt need to do so, since prayer brings help and peace. When you do something with your heart, you do it with love.

FINBAR: What did you think when you first got this interior vision of Our Lord and Our Lady?

JELENA: I didn't really think too much about it. I attached more importance to what 'Gospa' was saying.

FINBAR: What does 'Gospa' require of us?

JELENA: The first thing is that we undergo a conversion: change our lives and our hearts, and live the Gospel.

FINBAR: Why did the 'Gospa' choose you?

JELENA: She could have chosen anyone.

FINBAR: Do you know the six visionaries and visit them?

JELENA: Yes, we know each other very well. But we haven't all that much contact because they live some distance away.

FINBAR: What recommendations do you make to pilgrims?

JELENA: I can only say what 'Gospa' tells me in the messages. One day we asked Her what pilgrims should take away with them from Medjugorje. She said that, above all, they should change their lives for the better. That is the all-important thing. Also we should grow in faith and prayer – and ask God especially to give us inner peace.

FINBAR: Do you know the secrets? What will happen after the warnings? And what will the miraculous sign be?

JELENA: No, I don't. I know only what you do. And I don't know whether the sign is close at hand or still a long way off.

FINBAR: You say this is the last time 'Gospa' will appear on earth. Is that so?

JELENA: Yes.

FINBAR: Does 'last time' mean there will be no more Marian apparitions at all?

JELENA: I wonder about that too. 'Gospa' once said to us, 'If you have faith, you don't have to be afraid of anything. You know that Jesus is your friend and brother. So what is there to be afraid of?'

FINBAR: Therefore we must not fear?

JELENA: Exactly. But we have to do God's will.

FINBAR: Sometimes that's difficult!

JELENA: Yes. And, if we don't pray, it's almost impossible to do God's will. We must pray, otherwise faith will disappear. And, if we don't increase our amount of prayer, we'll always have a sort of fear. Faith is in danger because the devil is ever active. He's always on the alert and trying to cause us trouble.

FINBAR: So you believe in the devil's negative influence over us?

JELENA: Yes. To give an example: when we increase our prayer, he becomes angrier than ever and tries to upset us. But we should not forget, that with prayer, we are stronger than he is.

FINBAR: Have you personally felt the devil's negative influences?

JELENA: Yes. When I have not abandoned myself to God and I am doing my own will rather than His – that's when I make mistakes.

FINBAR: Do you always have a desire to pray?

JELENA: Yes. For me, prayer is repose. And I think it should be so for everyone. 'Gospa' has told me that we ought to find repose in prayer. When people do not pray, it's always because they're afraid of God. In prayer, the Lord wants to give us peace, security, joy.

FINBAR: Are we advised to say prayers that have been taught to us or to pray from our hearts?

JELENA: We should do both. We must pray from the heart – but also never omit to say the rosary or set prayers. It's a very beautiful thing when we can call God 'Our Father' and say that prayer.

FINBAR: It is easy to fall into a formalistic concept of prayer, that is to pray in the time, in the quantity, in the forms that one should, and believe in this way that one has carried out one's duty but without having met God. Some may feel discouraged because of their state and abandon prayer.

JELENA: I would not say that one prays well only when it is a joy to pray. Praying is necessary even when one feels disturbed. Our Lady says that prayer is nothing more than a great meeting with the Lord. It is not only to say one's prayers in order to do one's duty in this sense. She says that through this journey [in prayer] we can understand more and more. If one is distracted it means that one doesn't feel like praying. Instead, it is necessary to feel like it, and to pray to feel like it. Then Our Lady says that it is necessary to surrender to the Lord in everything that we do, in work, when studying with people, and in this way it will become easier to speak to God because one is less attached to everything.

FINBAR: For me it is difficult to pray. I pray but I never seem to reach the depth of prayer but have to do more and more.

JELENA: It is important that you abandon to the Lord these desires and disturbances of yours because Jesus says, 'I want you as you are.' If we were perfect we would not need Jesus. This desire to do more and more can certainly help us to pray better because it is necessary to understand that our entire life is a journey and it is necessary to go further and further ahead.

FINBAR: You are a student, as are many of our youngsters. Where do you find the time to pray?

JELENA: It comes to mind that Our Lady taught us not to measure time, and that prayer is really a spontaneous thing. Above all, I try to understand Our Lady as my real mother and

Jesus as my real brother, and so I don't just commit myself to fixed times for prayer which I could not manage. I try to understand that She really wants to help me all the time. When I feel tired I always try to pray the same, to really invoke Her because I know that if She did not help me, who else would help me? In this sense Our Lady is nearer to us when we are in difficulty and suffering.

FINBAR: How long do you pray in a day?

JELENA: Much depends on the day. Sometimes I pray for two or three hours, many times more, sometimes less. If I have many hours of school today, tomorrow I will find the time to do more. I always pray in the morning and evening, and during the day when I have time.

FINBAR: What impact does all this have on your friends at school? Do they tease you, or do they meet you halfway?

JELENA: As we are of different religions in my school, they are not very interested. But when they ask, I answer what they ask me. Actually they have never teased me. If, when speaking of these things we see that the way is a little hard, we never insist on speaking about them. We prefer to pray and to be an example as far as possible.

FINBAR: Has our Blessed Lady given you any indications about your future life?

JELENA: Our Blessed Lady has not told me of any particular choice, but She said: 'Pray, the Lord will enlighten you because [as She has explained to us] prayer is our only light.' So, it is important

to pray – then the rest He will make us understand.

FINBAR: You are studying now. What has Our Lady said
to you lately?

JELENA: Our Lady has said to thank the Lord for all that
He gives us, and really to accept every suffering
and every cross with love, and abandon oneself
to the Lord – to be so small because only when
we abandon ourselves to Him will He be able
to take us along the right road. I think that
when we force ourselves to go it alone, very
often we are only desperate. So, we have to
leave things to Him as He wants. Do just that,
to be ever smaller in front of Him, ever smaller.
Often the Lord sends us suffering to make us
smaller before Him. Let us understand that we
cannot do anything by ourselves.

FINBAR: When a person dies, can that person see us or
help us?

JELENA: Certainly, he can help us. For this reason Our
Blessed Lady says to pray for our dead all the
time, and our prayers will never be wasted
even if our dear one is in Heaven. Once Our
Lady said: 'If you pray for those souls, they will
pray for you in Heaven.' So, it is necessary to
pray for them.

FINBAR: But, is it really true that they can help us?

JELENA: Certainly. We say so in the Creed: 'I believe in
the communion of saints ...'

FINBAR: Our Blessed Lady has asked for prayer. Should
this be individual or communal prayer?

JELENA: Our Blessed Lady has said that personal prayer is very important in the beginning. Then She said that Jesus said to pray together. So, it is important to pray together also.

FINBAR: But what do you mean by prayer?

JELENA: Usually, when we are together we pray the rosary and general prayers, we read the New Testament and meditate but also many times we try to abandon ourselves with spontaneous prayer.

FINBAR: But, isn't even work prayer?

JELENA: Without doubt we haven't to abandon work, but to be able to do this well we have to pray. When I have prayed, even if things haven't gone very well, I still manage to feel the peace inside of me, otherwise I lose it at the first step. Even when I do lose peace, when I pray I have more patience to start again. Our Blessed Lady said, and also I have come to understand, that when I haven't prayed and I am too far from the Lord, and that happened often, I was not able to understand many things. I used to ask myself many questions, and in that way your entire life is in doubt. But, when you really pray, you receive security and this is very important. If we do not pray we cannot speak nor give witness to the authentic Christian life. We also are really responsible for our brothers. Our Blessed Lady said, 'Pray, and prayer will take you to the light' and it has really been like that. If one does not pray, one cannot understand and the words of others can only make us go further away; there is always this danger. Our Blessed Lady says: 'If you pray you can be sure.' She said: 'It is important to love, to do good to your neighbours, but first you must really give importance to the Lord. Pray because it is necessary to understand this by ourselves, that when we pray little and we have difficulty in praying, we can't even manage to help others – and then Satan really tempts us. Only the Lord keeps us from doing these things, and for this reason Our Lady says to us: 'Don't worry, He will take you along the true road.'

FINBAR: Has Our Lady asked for particular times in which to pray?

*The locutionary Jelena with Finbar
signing the prayer group's membership book at Holy Trinity.*

JELENA: Yes. She said in the morning, in the evening, and during the day when time is found. She didn't say you had to pray for hours, but the little that we do pray we should do so with love. And then, when you have more time, a day with more free time, then dedicate more time to prayer instead of perhaps dedicating it to those things that have less value.

FINBAR: Like today, which is Sunday, for example?

JELENA: Yes.

FINBAR: Does Our Lady tell you whether a particular thing is to be done, for example, for the sick, the suffering, or for the young?

JELENA: I cannot ask any of these things of Our Lady. The only thing I know is that there are organisations and initiatives taken for many things, but there is little prayer. More importance is given to doing than to praying – so the situation changes little. Our Lady says: 'It is necessary that we put ourselves in front of Jesus as well as helping others.' Our Lady has never told us to search for special initiatives to help others. Help in the way you have been given help. The first people who need our help are our family, our relatives, our neighbours, the ones whom we help less than all the others. A girl once told me that Mother Teresa said to young people: 'The family is a school of love.' So it is necessary to start from there. Our Blessed Lady always says this: 'Pray, especially in the families.'

Three Little Stories
from Jelena's Life

'The Nine Sermons'

This first story occurred during a visit of the former Archbishop Fran Franic from Split and Fr Slavko. During the conversation Jelena said she had something to give them. She left the room and returned with a sheet of paper on which she had written nine themes for preaching a Christmas novena and also a message. Jelena told her visitors that Our Lady had given them to her during her hour of prayer, just before they had arrived. The themes and messages are as follows:

1. Open your hearts because Jesus wants to dwell in them after Christmas.

2. To accept Christmas with love.

3. To purify yourself for Christmas.

4. From now on let Jesus be first in your hearts.

5. Let only Jesus give you love.

6. Let love be in your words.

7.   The God-Man who wants the whole world to be one has been born.

8.   To live with Jesus.

9.   Do not separate yourselves from Christmas.

The message was:

> Let the Church be fragrant with Christmas. Let Christmas be already on your doorstep. Purify your hearts and be pure receiving Christmas. Do not let luxury be more important at Christmas than Jesus who is being born. Receive Him with joyful hearts. Let everyone receive Christmas this way.

'The Birth of Jesus'

This second episode occurred when Jelena was twelve years old during the Christmas season of 1984. It was related to Fr Tomislav Vlasic, who recorded it as follows:

JELENA: A few days before Christmas a movie, *Ben Hur*, was playing in Čitluk and it was said Jesus was mentioned in it, how He was born and how He suffered. The movie was starting at 7 p.m. Mirjana and myself were going to church every evening because Our Lady has asked this of us, and the rosary and prayers after Mass. Because of that my dad said to me that I couldn't see the movie. I was sad for that reason.

   Then Our Lady said to me: 'Do not be sad. On Christmas I'll show you how Jesus was born.'

Those Christmas days an angel was appearing to me as in the previous year. This was how the vision went: I see an angel. Then he disappears and I see darkness. In the darkness I see St Joseph. He holds a staff in his hands. In that place there is some grass, and stones on the road, and a few houses around. Mary is on a mule. It looks like She is crying but She is not crying. She is sad. She says, 'I would be glad if someone would take us in for tonight, because I am tired.' Joseph says, 'Here are the houses, we will ask.' And they knock on the door. People open the door, and when they see Joseph and Mary they close it. That is repeated two or three times. When they start towards the other houses the lights begin disappearing in them. They are sad. Joseph says, 'There is an old house; surely no one sleeps in it. Surely it is abandoned.' And they go there. Inside there is one mule. They put their own mule alongside the manger. Joseph gathers some pieces of wood to make a fire. He also puts some hay on it but the fire consumes it immediately. So Mary is warmed by the mule. Mary cries and is very sad. Joseph feeds the fire. Suddenly I see Jesus in front of Mary. He smiled as if He were one year old.

He is joyful and it seems as if He is speaking. He waves his hands. Joseph comes to Mary and Mary says, 'Joseph this day of joy has come, but it would be better to pray, because there are people who do not allow Jesus to be born.' So they pray.

Suddenly, I see a little house only. It is lighted up a little bit. And then suddenly it becomes completely lighted up as in daytime, and the stars are in the skies. I see two angels above the stall. They hold a big banner, and written on it is: 'We glorify you, Lord!' Above it there is a big choir of angels. They sing and glorify God. Then I see the shepherds. They are weary, tired, and some are already sleeping. Some walk. The sheep and the lambs with them. One angel approaches them and says, 'Shepherds, hear the good news! God is born! You will find Him sleeping in a manger in the stall. Know that I am telling the truth.' Suddenly a large choir of angels joins them singing.

FR TOM.:   Did you look at this as in a movie?

JELENA: It looked real. I looked at that as I look at Our Lady.

Saint James Church, Medjugorje.

'Thank You'

The most moving moment in Jelena's apparitions was on Our Lady's two-thousandth birthday. In early August 1984, Our Lady gave the following message to Jelena:

> This message is dedicated to the Pope and to all Christians. Prepare the second millennium of my birth which will take place 5 August 1984. Throughout the centuries, I consecrated my entire life to you. Is it too much for you to consecrate three days for me. Do not work on that day, but take up the rosary and pray.

The Parish's Response

Fr Tomislav speaking the day after Our Lady's birthday said:

> I will explain what has happened during the last four days. On Thursday, Friday and Saturday most of the parishioners fasted on bread and water. Some people and families did not go to work. They only prayed. Many people fasted for the whole of the novena. Yesterday was the day of prayer and the whole of the parish prayed. It has been the happiest day of my life because I felt full of joy. This is my personal reason. Another reason is that as a priest, I have never seen so many miraculous conversions as during this time. All the priests who were hearing confessions agree. People really threw themselves into their confession asking how to mend their ways, what they had to do and were truly ready to change their lives. We have had some unexplainable cases of people on their way to the seaside feeling a force pushing them here to Medjugorje to pray and to go to confession. There

have been examples of deep confessions after a lapse of fifteen, thirty-five or forty years.

Yesterday and the day before, many young men and women came here in the deepest of faith to be consecrated to God and to Our Lady.

The reason for our happiness is that the visionaries say Our Lady is very joyful at this time. On all three days She said: 'I am very joyful, continue, continue, continue. Continue to pray and fast.' The visionaries say that Our Lady has never been as happy as She was yesterday. She was full of joy, just like a bud about to blossom, and said: 'Continue, continue. Open your hearts, ask God; and I will ask with you.'

Another moving moment of her apparitions was the following: the two young visionaries, Jelena and Mirjana, gave Our Lady a small Madonna (Child Mary) from Lourdes on our behalf and asked Her to bless it specially so we could have something by which to remember yesterday. Jelena said that Our Lady looked at it and started to weep, here usual tears were followed by tears of blood, transformed into tears of gold, and She said: 'Never in my life have I wept in sorrow, as in joy this evening. Thank you.' This is the reason why we are so happy.

The important matter for us priests now is what is happening at an interior level. As I said, we have seen a great many conversions and have been able to feel the peace in people and in their souls. Yesterday, I really understood what the Lord's day meant – not a day for tourism; we have transformed Sundays and feast days into sightseeing days. This is why we are in poor spirit. As I told you, I lived a true Lord's day because people had prepared themselves for it by fasting and prayer and prayed all day. So I asked the population of this village to go ahead for thirty-four days, because then we celebrate the Eucharistic Congress of the Croatian Church and, on the same day, 9 September, the Feast of the Cross on the hill here. I have asked people to transform Sundays into the Lord's day, into a day of prayer, if they want to feel this is truly the Day of the Lord.

I am lying when I say I have no time to pray. In the past few days, as you have seen, I have been very busy but, in spite of this, I have recited many rosaries because we decided to pray more and more. I took my rosary wherever I went – with the nuns, the people, in the car, and so I prayed all day. I told myself that I had been lying when I said I had no time to pray. After this, I felt purified within and other people, too, gave testimony to me of how they have been able to pray. For example, during these past few days, many families have not worked but prayed. Some young people asked their parents' permission to pray and set up tents in the woods; they took bread and water with them and prayed and fasted all day. There were some wonderful experiences.

Overcome with Joy
It was during this period that Jelena, overcome with joy exclaimed to the Blessed Mother, 'You are so beautiful.' Mary replied, 'I am beautiful because I love, If you want to be beautiful, love.'

Conversation with Marijana

Marijana Vasilj, born 5 October 1972, is one of the two girls who have the gift of inner locutions. On 19 March 1983, she began to receive messages from Our Lady in a similar way to the other locutionary, Jelena Vasilj.

FINBAR: Marijana, when did the Blessed Mother begin to speak to you?

MARIJANA: The first time was in March 1983.

FINBAR: Can you still remember how it was?

MARIJANA: I do remember. You know that Jelena heard the Blessed Mother's voice earlier than I did. We prayed together with Her every day. This continued for about two or three months. One day I did not go to pray. I went to a friend's house. Jelena then came and said that the Blessed Mother wants us to come and pray. At that time as I went along to pray I heard Her voice for the first time. Since then I hear the Blessed Mother's voice almost every day.

FINBAR: What is it like when the Blessed Mother speaks to you?

MARIJANA: It is a feeling, an inspiration, just like a voice of our conscience. Unlike the other six visionaries, we are not in ecstasy but in a very normal state. During the time the Blessed Mother speaks to us we feel deep peace and love which comes from within us.

FINBAR: When do you hear the Blessed Mother? Anytime at all or do you have special times?

MARIJANA: Only in prayer.

FINBAR: Always if you pray or only at certain times?

MARIJANA: Not in every prayer, but at least three times a week when the Blessed Mother gives messages to the prayer group. The Blessed Mother also gives messages for us [personally] or for others.

FINBAR: You mentioned the prayer group. The Blessed Mother appealed through you and Jelena to form a prayer group. Can you recall how it was at that time?

MARIJANA: I remember that the Blessed Mother wished, through Jelena, that we should build a youth prayer group. As we were ten and eleven years old at that time, we could not do it ourselves. We brought this wish to the priest, Fr Tomislav Vlasic. The priests announced it to the public and the youth followed. That was the beginning.

FINBAR: How many prayer groups have been founded by the Blessed Mother?

MARIJANA: Founded are [firstly] our prayer group [secondly] Ivan's prayer group and [thirdly] the one which was guided by Fr Slavko – whether this one was founded by the Blessed Mother, I do not know.

FINBAR: There is also the so-called small prayer group which built around you and Jelena. Does this group still meet? What instruction did this group receive?

MARIJANA: The small group meets once a month, but all their members are also in the big prayer group. Also, the messages for the small group are the same as the big group. If we look at the messages then we see that the Blessed Mother always invites us from one message to the other, to devotion to God, to prayer. The Blessed Mother wants us to be like a light for others – maybe also as an example for all who come here to Medjugorje.

FINBAR: Through whom did the Blessed Mother give messages to the big group which meets three times a week at the parish rectory? Through who does She now give the messages?

MARIJANA: At the beginning the Blessed Mother gave messages only through Jelena. For some time now She also gives messages through me to the group. I receive the message beforehand so that it can be read at the beginning of the prayers. The message is read during the prayer. Towards the end, at the time of the blessing Jelena receives a message.

FINBAR: What is the aim of these prayer groups in Medjugorje?

MARIJANA: As young people we should pray together, learn how to pray, learn to live according to our faith and how to come closer to God. In all this, She gives us full freedom to choose for ourselves what we want to do in life, but we should give the first place to prayer.

FINBAR: Marijana, do you only hear the Blessed Mother or do you also see Her too?

MARIJANA: Mostly I hear the Blessed Mother. Occasionally I also see Her in the form of inner visions. I never see the Blessed Mother with my physical eyes.

Note: The charism of Mirjana and Jelena is clearly different from the six main visionaries in Medjugorje.

FINBAR: How does the Blessed Mother appeal to you, to the prayer group and what messages does She give?

MARIJANA: We have already said it often. These messages are an appeal to pray, for devotion to God. I believe, above all, the Blessed Mother asks us to be examples for others through our lives and that we see Jesus in every person – that we see good and not only bad, and that we orientate ourselves according to the good. That's what She asks us for, what She requests of us. She says that She has come to help – not only us – but the whole world. I believe that we could work in this plan through our prayers, through being an example, through our lives.

FINBAR: The Blessed Mother invites us always to prayer. How much time do you take yourself for prayers? What do you recommend to others who meet in prayer groups?

MARIJANA: The Blessed Mother desires that we pray three hours daily, if possible. Sometimes I can't manage to pray for three hours, but I do it as often as I can. The Blessed Mother has expressed the special meaning of morning prayers. She says that we should begin the day with God. There are days when I pray less than three hours, and there are days when I pray more than three hours.

FINBAR: Tell us about your everyday routine, especially when you are not in school?

MARIJANA: After waking up we pray our morning prayers in the family. Then we go to do the work which we have to do. A lot of time I spend with the pilgrims who come. After that, when I have time, I pray. Then I go to church. Three times a week after the Holy Mass our prayer group meets to pray.

FINBAR: Did the Blessed Mother give messages through you and Jelena for the entire parish or for the whole world?

MARIJANA: Earlier messages also used to come to the parish and for the world. Because the Blessed Mother requested that the prayer group remain within itself, it resulted in such that the messages remained in the group.

FINBAR: What do you think of the development – the present situation – of Medjugorje.

MARIJANA: I think for a long time now a tepid phase has come in here. It manifests itself – first of all with myself – in relation to prayer and other things. The Blessed Mother appealed to us that we should be the way we were in the beginning of the apparitions, which means that the splendour of prayer should return. We should not turn too much to materialistic things. The Blessed Mother's greatest wish is that in our lives prayer should have the first place.

FINBAR: What do you recommend to people who come to you and want to talk to you?

MARIJANA: The Blessed Mother says for all those who come here to Medjugorje, that they should open their hearts. They should try to give themselves totally to God. All that they feel and experience here they should take back home. And when they get back home they should be examples for those who do not believe and do not pray. It is very important that when they get back home that they should continue to pray and fast.

FINBAR: Did the Blessed Mother lead you to Jesus?

MARIJANA: The Blessed Mother told us that each prayer should be a conversation with God – we can accept Jesus as our friend, as somebody who is totally close to us – and that we should be bound to Him through prayer. Especially important should be our prayers from the heart. Whatever we experience, all our problems and difficulties, we should give to God, to Jesus. The Blessed Mother invites us always to prayer in front of the cross. She says we should accept the cross with love.

FINBAR: Marijana, thank you for this conversation, and your prayers.

The young locutionaries Jelena and Marijana.

A Testimony
from Marija Duganozic, member of the prayer group

We have seen how the villagers in Medjugorje could participate in the prayer group, providing they agreed to the four-year commitment. One of the participants, Marija Duganozic (not one of the visionaries), who was born in 1967 gives us the following testimony of her years in Our Lady's prayer group.

You surely already know that it was really Our Lady's will that this group be formed. In our parish there was already a prayer group even before the apparitions began, but it was a normal group as can be found in most parishes. However, in 1983, Our Lady really called. She wanted to form Her own group in order to guide it in a particular way.

Our Lady wanted the group. She gave messages through the two small locutionaries, Jelena and Marijana. At once She asked for a commitment from each member of the group. Each one had to decide yes or no. Forty-five persons remained. There were others who did not feel up to it, but Our Lady said that each of us should feel no more important than the others, that they could continue well with their lives.

So, freely we decided to remain for four years without making a choice for life. We were invited to daily prayer for three hours, afterwards four hours, and daily Mass, and fasting twice a week – even three times when She asked for it. Our Lady desired right from the beginning that there should always be a priest with us, and asked that we meet once a week. Our Lady always gave a message through Jelena on which we meditated after the meeting.

As time passed, Our Lady asked the group to meet twice a week and then three times a week.

Second Weekly Meeting

So, Our Lady told us to meet twice a week. Just in this period She told us to pray seven Our Fathers, Hail Marys and Glory Bes and the prayer to the Holy Spirit for the Bishop. At this second meeting we would bring everything in our hearts, as a rule of life, on how to resolve a problem with prayer. Many things were said here when there were many difficulties with the Bishop, but Our Lady said: 'Pray.' So, now we don't discuss it anymore. We pray and that's all.

This second meeting is a little shorter than the others, but when it started during the Year of Peace 1985, Our Lady asked us to do something as a group for peace in the world – a prayer, a small act of charity. We decided at this meeting to add an Our Father, Hail Mary and Glory Be. We continued for a short while with two messages a week, but then Our Lady wanted even a third meeting.

Third Weekly Meeting

The third meeting in the week was a little different from the others. It is more of a dialogue among us. Our Lady, who led the group, saw that in order for the persons to be a real community, prayer was not enough. She desired that we be open, talk together, meet each other, because many problems are created when people do not meet each other.

Difficulties in Prayer Groups

Our Lady asked that at the beginning of Lent we choose a person from the group with which to speak, to be together with, and with whom to share this experience of Lent. She told us that we have to seek with our eyes the person in the group who is furthest away from us and with whom we have the most difficulty. At this moment we really felt as though God touched our life because just in that moment we had to meet the truth. How difficult it was to say to a person that perhaps I didn't like you, or that you are the furthest away. It was difficult to accept this truth, but at the time we felt the presence of Our Lady and especially the grace to deal with the difficulties at the time. With a smile we met each other and, being together, we saw how all these people had a hidden treasure to be discovered. Then Our Lady asked us during the following weeks to take another person, always starting with the person sitting opposite in the group so that we had to go around in a circle with the people of the group.

The Secret of Being a Real Community

I can say that this experience is really the most powerful of all because the community could only feel that way by meeting with everybody with the feeling that we want to be open with everybody in the same way. Afterwards, the barriers between us disappeared. We really see that we hold on to this rule. When we do not get along with a person we have to meet with them because the problem does not get resolved in any other way. Life stays empty.

Then, as many times, as a group, we experienced difficulty, different trials, but everything has to be resolved, cleared up. Our Lady lets us do this by ourselves, and then afterwards a priest explains. A great deal of time is taken up for prayer for understanding.

On another occasion Our Lady explained why persons being together do not feel together in spirit. In fact one feels like praying for one thing, but another feels like thanking, another feels like asking for a blessing – in that way prayer is not united. Our Lady suggested that one person starts to pray, and another follows, but many times we have not been able to obey this.

Rules For Prayer
Our Lady has given us four points for prayer.

Feel Forgiven
It is my confession, my meeting with God, my examination of conscience. She told us that it is impossible for one to pray unless one is at peace with God and with one's brother. We have to feel that the Lord has forgiven us. We have to be very humble and open before God. We don't have to hide anything. She said that many times we stop thinking that the Lord

has forgiven us because we don't believe in His love. Our Lady said: 'Dear children, don't think that it is like that. The Lord forgives you at once, from the moment you are sorry … so you don't have to despair.' She told us that God forgives at once, that only two minutes are enough. She said that just two minutes to think of the past, even the smallest sin or even the greatest sin, but do not let time pass after the sin without asking for forgiveness because Satan will take advantage of this pause and will take you into evil. Then She told us that we just have to be sons brought up by the Father who loves us even though we are not perfect. She says that every time we start to pray, alone or in a group, we have to remember the importance of asking for forgiveness and to feel that the Lord has forgiven us.

Pray for Ourselves and Everyone

Then Our Lady told us that we have to leave a pause for silence to be able to be more meditative and more attentive. Then we should pray for our own intentions and for all those who have come to the group, and to pray spontaneously for others and for everyone.

Give Thanks

Our Lady said that the moment of thanksgiving is very important. She said that really we are a generation that is not capable of thanking because we think that all we have is through our own merit or of our own doing. Instead, She says, all we have and are, is a gift from God. Therefore we should always thank Him for everything – for what God gives and for what He takes. This is just the moment in which each person, while thanking God, should also show their faith in the Father because we believe in His plan for us, either when He takes or gives us something.

The Blessing

This is very important. Our Lady spoke to us once about the blessing and its importance and that we shouldn't end the meeting without God's blessing. Even before, we had ended the meeting with the blessing but we didn't ask for it with faith. It was a normal gesture to end prayer, that's all. Our Lady explained to us that the blessing of God does not guarantee that nothing evil will happen to us, nor that the cross will not come to us. But it is a guarantee that we really are not alone. God is with us and will help us. For this She has suggested that we ask more than once each day for God's blessing, and above all when we think of a sin we have committed. Just when we are far from God that is the moment when we have to ask for the blessing again. She has told us that we can lose the blessing if we build our daily life far from that which God wants of us. At the meetings She has suggested that we pray for the blessing and sing the Our Father.

We don't have to try to make sacrifices, but the small things in our lives done with love are great things.

Marija Pavlovic
Visionary

Marija Pavlovic was born in Medjugorje on 1 April 1965. Gentle Marija, small and lithe like a little doe, was not present on Podbrdo Hill on the first evening of the apparitions (24 June 1981). The next day she accompanied her five young friends and saw Our Lady, and so became one of the six visionaries.

I would like to quote here from a talk Marija gave to several thousands of people during a tour of Russia, just after the fall of the communist regime. The church she was in had been used by the communists as a museum and pictures of Lenin and Marx were still hanging on the walls.

Marija assured the congregation that she entrusted everyone to Our Lady and she would present Russia to Her everyday, she continued:

> Our Lady arrived as Queen of Peace and asked us to pray for that peace which can only come from God. First in our hearts, then together with the family, peace then descends on the family. We can pray for peace in the world. Our Lady asked that we live more like Christians, to go to church and not to leave the Blessed Sacrament alone. Our Lady asked that 'prayer groups start up'. One of the fruits of Medjugorje

is that many prayer groups have begun and, united, they pray together. The Bishop and Fr Leonard have already said many lovely things. 'I will tell you how we see Our Lady ... '

Marija summarised the history of the apparitions and said:

We were not children that prayed much. We were just like all other children. But then we understood that Our Lady wanted us to take the matter seriously and that we start praying. Our Lady told us that She wished to guide us, to school us in prayer. She asked that we put God before everything else in our lives. So, we started praying. We saw that our habits, at times, were rather heathen and we had to change them. Our Lady once said, 'When you are in church you are good and holy, but outside of the church you are like heathens.' She asked us to give testimony wherever we happen to be, like a school. So we started changing and things around us starting changing too. Our Lady helped us to understand what is good and what is bad.

She gave us complete freedom every time. Our Lady helps us like a teacher, but She loves us like a mother. The eyes of Our Lady, which we see every day, help us to understand things with depth because they are azure and deep, like the ocean. Once we asked Her why She was so beautiful, and She replied, 'I am beautiful because I love.' So we decided to love more, too.

Through Her messages, Our Lady calls all of us to choose the way to holiness. She said that She wants all of us to become holy. Mary showed us that there is another life, and She said that the only thing we can take with us to the other life, to Heaven, is holiness.

She said at various times that this is the moment of grace. We must pray, and offer our work as a prayer. Our Lady always repeats 'Pray more'. I want to invite also, all of you to pray and be united to us.

New Year's Night, 2001, the first night of the new century. The visionary Marija, sharing Our Lady's Message with pilgrims on Podbrdo after her apparition, said:

Our Lady was Joyful. She came accompanied by five angels. She prayed over us and I recommended all of you present, all your intentions and all the sick people present in a special way. Our Lady gave this message:

'My dear children, tonight I desire for you to be with me, now that Satan is unchained I invite you to be close to me. I desire you to consecrate to my heart and to the heart of my Son.'

She blessed all of us with Her motherly blessing with the sign of the cross. She said go in peace, my dear children.

Conversation with Marija

A Calling to Holy Mass

Fr Slavko, who was Marija's spiritual director, recorded this beautiful conversation, which explores Marija's thoughts on the meaning of Our Lady's messages for herself and for the youth of the world.

FR SLAVKO: Marija, what would you say to young people who are searching for God, and do not know where to find Him, or where to look for Him?

MARIJA: They should do what Our Lady is telling us to do. Everyone has to make a personal decision to put God in the first place in one's life. Naturally, through prayer and by following the messages which Our Lady is giving us here in Medjugorje, we will recognise what is the will of God for each of us, and so for young people too.

FR SLAVKO: What, in fact, is Our Lady recommending? And please remember, people who are going to read this interview are probably hearing about this for the first time.

MARIJA: The main messages that Our Lady is calling us to live are as follows: Peace, Prayer, Conversion, Fasting, Penance and Holy Mass. On the 25th of each month, She gives messages for all who wish to follow the way, regardless of where they live, or where they work, or at what they work.

FR SLAVKO: What would you say to the young people who find Holy Mass boring?

MARIJA: I think, and Our Lady is also telling us, that the centre of our lives is the Holy Mass, and She is ever recommending the Holy Mass to us. I am sure that if everyone understood that the Holy Mass is a meeting with God, they could not possibly find it boring.

FR SLAVKO: Did you ever feel that way during Holy Mass, that it was too long or boring or something like that?

MARIJA: Yes, in the beginning, of course, when I found it very difficult to understand. But when I began to pray, then I started to understand the importance and greatness of Holy Mass.

FR SLAVKO: I know you have said on one occasion if you were asked to choose between the apparitions and the Eucharist, you would choose the moment of the Eucharist.

MARIJA: For sure I would, because Our Lady is always calling us to Holy Mass, and She said that the Holy Mass is the centre of our lives. So if the Holy Mass is the centre of our lives, and we meet with the living God in the Eucharist, why then would I not choose God and meeting with Him?

FR SLAVKO: It seems to me that the purpose of Our Lady's presence is to educate you and all the people to participate in the Holy Mass?

MARIJA: Yes, that is the main idea that Our Lady is putting before us – many of the messages are calling people to Holy Mass.

FR SLAVKO: You mentioned once, I clearly remember, that if you were very tired coming to the apparition, when it was over, you felt strong enough to embrace the whole world. Does that mean that if this happens to you after an apparition, it would be even more true after Holy Mass?

MARIJA: We always feel that way when we go to an apparition. It is some special grace. And the same is true during Holy Mass – God is giving Himself to us in some special way. Naturally, if we are Christians, we should be aware of the fact that God is always with us. But during Holy Mass, He is with us in a special way, when He gives Himself to us in the form of His Body and Blood. We always feel enormous happiness and joy, because of the fact that God is giving Himself to us. That is the most important happening in our faith.

FR SLAVKO: In one of the messages, Our Lady said through you: 'I wish that your lives become the Holy Mass, and that the Holy Mass becomes your life.' How would you explain that to young people, when they read the message? Would you mind adding your own explanation to it?

MIRJANA: I will say what Our Lady says. We certainly feel that the Holy Mass is our life, because then we meet with God and God is for us our life. By offering to God all our efforts and problems during Holy Mass, we will fulfill what She asks from us.

FR SLAVKO: Good. How did you feel and live through the fast and prayers? What would you say to young people today who are beginning to pray and fast?

MARIJA: Always on the day of the fast, I felt some great grace. Not only because on that day I did not need to work, or cook, but because I had much more time for praying, and I felt God closer, almost as if He were not anymore in the clouds, but I could physically feel Him around, on that day which is full of special grace.

FR SLAVKO: Did you feel the same way in the beginning, or were you doing it only to obey Our Lady?

MARIJA: It was very difficult in the beginning. It is always difficult when one has to make a decision.

FR SLAVKO: If young people today cannot begin with the fast, what would you recommend them to do for a start, to give up something?

MARIJA: Our Lady specially recommended that we give up things like television, cigarettes, some other bad habits, some things to which we are addicted.

FR SLAVKO: Marija, in your great unselfish love, you donated one of your kidneys to your brother, and as a consequence of that you are still weak and not completely well. There are young people who are not in good health, injured at work, or born sick. Let them hear the message about the fast. What would you tell them about the fast, now when you are a convalescent yourself?

MARIJA: What I feel the sacrifice God sent us gives me great joy. I discovered a great joy in the sacrifice that I made to God for my brother. This is very special to me. It is difficult to explain the pleasure I felt in being able to give something to God for my brother. This is very special to me. It is difficult to explain the pleasure I felt in being able to give something to God some sacrifice whatever it might be!

There is so much around. Take only the souls in Purgatory, it is so important for them. One small sacrifice of ours could help souls go to Heaven, and we are not aware of the fact most of the time. For that reason, I would ask everyone to take seriously the sacrifices they have in life – 'crosses' we used to call them – and offer them to God for the souls in Purgatory, or for the sick, or for the hungry. There are so many that we can choose from.

FR SLAVKO: Those people who are ill, how could they fast? How would you advise them to do it?

MARIJA: They could decide to pray more on that day. They could choose some other form of fasting besides bread and water. They could give up some of their habits. Ill people can often give way to complaining, so on that day they could decide not to grumble about their pains.

FR SLAVKO: What helped me the most: Our Lady directs that we decide for the school of prayer. Whenever I pray less, I feel I can give less. When I pray more, I feel I can bring God to people.

MARIJA: That means that not only the apparitions help us, as they are among the special graces that God is giving us. At the same time, our meeting with God [in prayer] is equally important in our lives. Our Lady is giving us complete freedom. The apparitions do not restrict us. We shall have our freedom in deciding.

FR SLAVKO: I feel that you have a special right to call young people to make sacrifices, as you yourself have shown an heroic example in your sacrifice for others. Tell them something about it now.

MARIJA: Certainly, I feel this as a gift. Every time I see my brother, I feel the greatest joy and a motherly spirit that I sense in my heart and that is caring for him. I feel that is a gift God gave me, and so every time I see him I am conscious that I saved him, and I am aware that if I did not do that [donate a kidney] he would not be alive today. It is a very, very big matter for me, a great joy.

FR SLAVKO: So it means that we should, by example, encourage others to do good things?

MARIJA: From my experience I know that whenever I gave something to someone, I brought joy to that person. The same happened when I gave life to my brother with a gift of one of my kidneys. That is a great thing, and I feel great joy in my heart for that.

FR SLAVKO: We are having this conversation just before the time of apparition. Will you recommend to Our Lady all young people who are going to read this?

MARIJA: I will, this evening. During the apparition I will recommend all of them to Our Lady.
I hope that this year will be a constant encouragement for them to be converted.

FR SLAVKO: What would you advise those young people to do, who already follow the messages and pray, but are aware that their friends do not pray and continue in a bad way of life?

MARIJA: To pray for them and to try and give them to God. And to try and get them to accept the messages according to which Our Lady is calling us to live.

FR SLAVKO: Good. One more question. Our Lady told us some time ago to think about the quotation from St Matthew's Gospel (6:24–34); She told us through Jelena. We are to surrender to God, and not to worry about material things, that God will take care of everything. Young people find it difficult to search first for God's Kingdom and not for material things. What would you tell them about that?

MARIJA: Naturally, we often look at things in a human way, and we find ourselves tied to our security, and we are afraid to lose it. If we really want to decide for God, then material things are a help to survive, and we should use them for good deeds. If we think that way, the car is not going to be a God for us, we will not put it and other material things in the place of Our Lady said we should put God in the first place. So with regard to material things, they are not as important as the spiritual things and as God.

FR SLAVKO: I would say that you are really explaining the last message from April. Through you, Our Lady said in that message to put everything you have in God's hands.

MARIJA: Surely. In that moment in which we are ready to give God everything, at that same moment we will have everything. I feel all the time that God is giving us great graces.

FR SLAVKO: I know that one journalist asked you can a person who has apparitions ever forget God?

MARIJA: Ah, I would not know! I am convinced that each of us has total freedom and can decide to be pagans if we want to, despite the gift that is given to us. Our Lady assures us of total freedom, and She said in one of Her messages: 'I praise the freedom the Lord is giving to you.' I really feel that we are totally free.

FR SLAVKO: When the young people hear all this, and still continue to destroy their lives taking drugs and alcohol, what would you tell them? For example, if you met somebody you know who is not listening to Our Lady's messages, what would you tell that person?

MARIJA: I would give the person Our Lady's blessing.

FR SLAVKO: How would you do that?

MARIJA: On one occasion Our Lady gave us a gift of a special blessing that we could give to others. When She told us about the blessing, She said She was giving us Her special motherly blessing, which can change and convert people, change their attitude of heart and life.

FR SLAVKO: Would it be your advice to parents to look after their children better, to be converted, and not to live in sin?

MARIJA: Surely! At the same time we have to pray for them. Changes happen. There is the example of St Augustine. His parents prayed for him. His mother gave a great example to our Church, as with her prayers she brought about his conversion to God.

FR SLAVKO: So that means that aggression and anger [with children] would not be helpful?

MARIJA: Our Lady is always telling us to give example to each other, young to their parents, and the parents to their children, and in that way to help each other.

FR SLAVKO: Do you have a special duty towards a priest?

MARIJA: I have felt for a long time that Our Lady has given me a special gift for priests. I often say how they asked me for advice and I didn't know what to say to them. After a long time had passed Our Lady asked me to pray and to offer a particular sacrifice for them. Often boys also confided in me that they wanted to become friars or priests and wanted to have me as their spiritual mother. All this was strange to me. Then I saw that as Mary had given to each a particular calling, She had given me a particular message for priests and also how to advise them. Upon meeting a priest I saw how it was easier to speak and how he was more open after we had spoken together. I saw how Our Lady desires the spiritual growth of each of us but, above all, of priests because She has always said that they are Her chosen sons ... And many times I see how priests do not really possess this value that Mary speaks of. She speaks of priesthood as being a great and beautiful thing which I don't find in all priests. My greatest prayer at this time is just this: to help priests discover the value of priesthood because even they do not know this, and we see here that only through prayer can it be discovered. Often we say to pray for them and nothing more than this. But, every day Our Lady calls us to grow more, to convert ourselves and to walk more and more along the path of holiness. It is hard to find a group of priests like this and I saw as Mary's plan the Venetian group from Brazil in January. Now I see that as Mary asked for a Year of Youth and desires that we form prayer groups, so priests have to be their spiritual leaders. In this way the Year of Youth is the Year of Priests because priests cannot be without youth and the Church cannot be renewed without them. Also youth cannot be without priests.

So Our Lady invites us to be converted. She has also mentioned one of our big problems:

> Your hearts are still taken up by earthly things
> and they worry you.

This is so true, we cannot pray if a lot of things worry us. Fr Slavko gives as an example: 'When studying, if you are just a bit concerned about your exams, you can study well. But if you become over concerned, you get completely seized with fear and cannot study. You are unable to study because both your mind and heart are distressed.'

If these are trials and events that worry us so much we are unable to pray with our heart, and so Our Lady invites us to be converted to prayer and to fasting. One frees the heart by fasting. I have much evidence of people who tell me: 'When I fast I can pray better, it is easier and I can pray more deeply.' Therefore, if we want to follow the messages, to pray with the heart and to have the joy that prayer can offer us, then we see that we have to fast in order to be able to abandon ourselves to God.

In this message, Our Lady said:

> I know that you are tired ... because you do not know how to abandon yourselves to me.

She said in a message after Easter:

> I invite you to prayer. Pray and you will overcome all tiredness.

For all of us, prayer should be a living encounter with the Lord, with Jesus Christ. He said: 'All of you come to me and I will help you.' One can, therefore, also understand this message in a physical sense; we can also rest in prayer.

All those who question what the sense of living, of suffering, is are tired. This is tiredness; and this message shows us that we can overcome it by prayer. From experience there, I can tell you: many who have begun to pray have been able to be reconciled with themselves, to find the meaning of life, of suffering and of everything else.

If we want to solve all our problems we must pray. Our Lady said in a message:

> Pray and you will find the greatest joy and the solution to all the most difficult situations.

Marija said that Our Lady has asked the prayer group to offer up to Her, every Wednesday, even the smallest thing, every difficulty, offer everything for Her intention. Marija said:

> When we did this, offered everything for Her intention, we immediately felt that our Blessed Lady had already taken these things and had

offered them up to Jesus. We must offer everything to Our Lady, including our sufferings, even our distress, our worries, our fears, everything, and then with prayer and fasting we will succeed more and more every day in this total abandonment.

A Call to All the World

Early in 1984 Our Lady said through Jelena that it was Her wish for all the parishioners of Medjugorje to come to the church on a weekday, so that She might give them direction in their spiritual lives. The priests with the people decided that this would take place on a Thursday; one reason being that they had exposition of the Blessed Sacrament on that evening.

The first meeting took place on 1 March and, on that occasion, Our Lady gave the first message to the parish through Marija:

> Dear children, I have chosen this parish in a special way because I want to guide you and protect you by love. Thank you for coming. May more of you come each time and stay close to my Son and I. I will give you a message each Thursday.

She has continued in this way each Thursday to give a message. I will only give you a brief summary of Our Lady's messages. Once She expressed the desire that all the parishioners be truly converted so that this Medjugorje community could become a source of conversion for all those who come here. She stressed the importance of the adoration of the Blessed Sacrament, the Veneration of Our Lord's wounds especially His side wound. Once She said:

Stop talking, but pray for the unity of the parish because my Son and I have a special plan connected with it.

Through Jelena, also at the first meeting of the parish, She gave this message:

Every Thursday, reread and put into practice the passage from the Gospel of St Matthew 6:24–34: A man cannot be the slave of two masters! Do not be worried: look at the birds of the air, make it your first care to find the Kingdom of God…

Later on you will realise that this passage of the Gospel has not been chosen by Our Lady at random, but because it reflects the meaning of peace as spoken of by Her. That same evening She said to Jelena:

Every Thursday, those who smoke should give it up at least on that day, those who drink alcohol give that up and others can give up some other pleasure, and if there are some generous people amongst you, they can also fast.

On Holy Thursday, She said:

Share my feelings; pray, pray, pray.

On 21 March She said to Jelena:

Today I am rejoicing with all my angels. The first part of the programme has been accomplished.

Then She paused and wept, saying:

> I do not know what to say. There are many
> people who live in sin! Here amongst you too,
> there are some people who are piercing my
> heart. Pray and fast for them.

The following day, 22 March, She said to Jelena:

> Yesterday I told you that the first part of my
> programme has already been accomplished;
> now turn to the second part by fasting and
> prayer so that this part, too may be accom-
> plished.

The Whole World is my Parish

As we have said, Marija was the chosen instrument to
convey this weekly lesson or message to the parish and the
world. She would receive it from Our Blessed Mother
during the regular daily apparition at 6.40 p.m. The priests
would later convey its contents, together with a homily or
reflection to those gathered in church. Over the years,
millions of devotees throughout the world now wait in
great expectation of Our Lady's message and strive to live
it to various degrees, each according to his/her calling and
commitment, whether it be lay person, priest or religious,
family or prayer group.

This programme for renewal continued on a weekly
basis for a total of one hundred and fifty weeks. Step by
loving step, in stages of proximity then weeks each, the
Mother of God called all of us, (yes, you also, dear reader)
to a special close relationship with Herself and Jesus, Her
Beloved Son. She called us to pray to the Holy Spirit,
especially for the spirit of prayer and fasting, always

encouraging our growth in the gift of prayer and love.

Then in the message of 8 January 1987, Our Lady said:

> Dear children! I want to thank you for your every response to my messages. Especially, dear children, thank you for all the sufferings and prayers you have offered me. Dear children, I want to continue giving you messages no longer every Thursday but on the 25th of each month. The time has come when what my Lord wanted has been fulfilled. From now onwards I give you less messages but I will continue to be with you.
>
> Therefore, dear children, I beg you, listen to my messages and live them, so that I can guide you.
>
> Dear children, thank you for your response to my call.

On the 24 November 2000, after a life of faithful service, Fr Slavko was called to his eternal reward.

Part of Our Lady's message to Marija on the following evening was:

'Today your brother Slavko has been born into Heaven.'

Fr Slavko Barbaric (1946–2000)

Monthly Messages

The first of the monthly messages was on the 25 January 1987 when Our Lady said:

You have a role in God's plan

> Dear children! Behold, also today I want to call you to start living a new life as of today. Dear children, I want you to comprehend that God has chosen each one of you, in order to use you in His great plan for the salvation of mankind. You are not able to comprehend how great your role is in God's design. Therefore, dear children, pray so that in prayer you may be able to comprehend what God's plan is in your regard. I am with you in order that you may be able to bring it about in all its fullness.
>
> Thank you for having responded to my call.

Then on 25 February 1987:

The way of conversion, a way of joy

> Dear children! Today I want to wrap you all in my mantle and lead you all along the way of conversion. Dear children, I beseech you, surrender to the Lord your entire past, all the evil that has accumulated in your hearts. I want

each one of you to be happy, but in sin nobody can be happy. Therefore, dear children, pray, and in prayer you shall realise a new way of joy. Joy will manifest in your hearts and thus you shall be joyful witnesses of which I and my Son want from each one of you. I am blessing you. Thank you for having responded to my call.

These monthly messages of exhortation continue. Our Blessed Mother is untiring in Her efforts to bring us to a state of holiness. She once said:

Dear children! My invitation that you live the messages I give you is a daily one, especially little children, because I want to draw you closer to the heart of Jesus. Therefore, little children, I am inviting you today to the prayer of consecration to Jesus, my dear Son, so that each of your hearts may be His; and then I'm inviting you to consecration to my Immaculate Heart. I want you to consecrate yourselves as persons, as families, and as parishes, so that all belongs to God through my hands. So, dear little children, pray that you may comprehend the greatness of this message, which I am giving you. I do not want anything for myself, rather, all for the salvation of your souls. Satan is strong and therefore, you little children, by constant prayer, press tightly to my motherly heart.

Thank you for responding to my call.

Ivan
Visionary

Ivan Dragicevic, a fine looking young man with a tendency to be serious, especially when speaking about the 'Gospa' and Her messages, was born in Bijakovici, Medjugorje on 25 May 1965. Ivan has been given the special task by Our Lady to bring Her messages to young people and encourage the formation of prayer groups throughout the world.

Let us look now at the content of a very perceptive and informative conversation between Ivan and his spiritual director, Fr Slavko Barbaric.

FR SLAVKO: Ivan, what can you recommend to young people searching for God, when they do not know where to turn?

IVAN: When we speak about young people, then we have to look at the wider concept; we must look deeper. We must ask in what circumstances did they grow up? What did their parents offer by way of advice? Did they give them their love and their time? Did they pray with them? Was there unity in their family, and were their parents open with their children? Those are the kind of things without which a family cannot function.

FR SLAVKO: What if there isn't a good upbringing in the family, but yet the young people are searching for God, and don't know where to turn?

IVAN: Today priests should give themselves, particularly to young people. Today this is especially true if the parents are chasing what is passing in life, like material things. That's why many young people lose themselves, they are left to fend for themselves, they are alone. Young people ought to help each other, together with the priests.

FR SLAVKO: So you mean a young person seeking God should go to a priest, or meet with another young person of the same age, who has already found God?

IVAN: The best way is to go to a priest, who will give good advice that can release the doubts and fears of young people. The priest should also contact the youth's parents.

FR SLAVKO: So what can you recommend, Ivan, to young people who find Holy Mass boring?

IVAN: That's a difficult question. Today not just young people but many grown-ups as well go to Holy Mass just to be seen. Sometimes they do not approach Holy Mass as the faith teaches: to listen to the Gospel and to live the Gospel.

FR SLAVKO: Did you ever feel that Holy Mass was boring?

IVAN: Nobody is perfect, and always in man there exists weakness, even at Holy Mass, as well as with other things in life.

FR SLAVKO: So was it boring at times?

IVAN: Yes.

FR SLAVKO: What does that mean to you now?

IVAN: For me now, Holy Mass means a precious moment in my life, and an act of faith, which cannot be replaced by anything. Not just Mass, but Confession and Holy Communion too, because after all they make me feel light and relaxed. I mean I feel this way after prayer.

FR SLAVKO: So, Mass is an unavoidable fact in your life?

IVAN: I like to see the Mass as the spiritual food which gives people special strength and power, if approached in the proper way. And after Mass, you can feel that your day is started and finished with Holy Mass, especially if you add a prayer of thanks-giving.

FR SLAVKO: Compared with now, what did you think of prayer and fasting before the apparitions started?

IVAN: Before the first apparition, my parents told me that I should fast on Friday, but I did it only before Easter. And I can truly say that I never prayed like now. Before I just prayed with my parents, but I was merely moving my lips without any thought.

FR SLAVKO: What would you say to young people who have just begun to pray and fast?

IVAN: When I speak to pilgrims about praying and fasting, I repeat that it is not necessary to force themselves. The most important thing for young people is to pray with the heart, with meditation and with hope, and with a firm decision to be persistant.

FR SLAVKO: Can you tell us now has your relationship with God developed? Does the Bible help you?

IVAN: You have to note the difference between the life before and after the first apparition. During these years the most important thing is not just seeing Our Lady, but doing what She wants.

FR SLAVKO: Did Our Lady say we should read the Bible?

IVAN: Yes, and She also told us to keep it in a visible place in the house, so that everybody cannot only see it but read it.

FR SLAVKO: What can you tell young people who say it is hard to believe in God?

IVAN: Surely we should ask ourselves why are young people distant from God, and look for reasons. When somebody gives himself to

God, some things become more important to him and other things become unimportant. This means that we must fulfil our part and God will give us everything. It doesn't mean we don't have to work at it. Young people look for passing things in life, so that God is forgotten. Later when we get sick or grow old, we will understand what is the most important thing in our lives.

FR SLAVKO: Tell us about Our Lady's love?

IVAN: It is very difficult to describe Our Lady's love. Whenever I meet Her I feel very relaxed. I want to say that Our Lady's love is so great, not just for us visionaries but for everyone in the world. Just a few days ago Our Lady said: 'You are always asking for new messages. Why do you need new messages, if you do not try to live those I have given you?'

FR SLAVKO: Tell me, how important is it for you to be a member of a prayer group?

IVAN: In this time of youth I can tell you being a member of a prayer group is one great experience. A new time of human fulfilment is opening up. I get so close with prayer [in the prayer group] and there I can see my way of life. I cannot imagine my spiritual growth without my prayer group.

FR SLAVKO: Every time you see Our Lady is it a new experience? Do you sometimes feel sad after an apparition, or are you always happy?

IVAN: Every meeting with Our Lady is full of joy and endless satisfaction. Our Lady is not just sad, She is crying. Her face says enough.

FR SLAVKO: Can you remember one particular sad or happy expression on Her face?

IVAN: For me, the best experience of meeting Our Lady was the one at the very beginning.

FR SLAVKO: When Our Lady gives messages during the apparitions, do you think She is conscious of all the problems of young people?

IVAN: She did not say without good reason that this year was to be a year for young people. She said that the year of youth was to be from 15 August last year to 15 August this year. She mentioned all the problems of youth: drugs, alcohol and so on. She spoke very much about the prayer group in the messages She gave to me. She wants young people to come together to meet each other, and parents and priests to join with them, so that there is communication between all. She wants priests to organise prayer groups in their own parishes. The leader of a prayer group can also be a lay person but one spiritually mature. Best he should work closely with a priest.

FR SLAVKO: What can you say to young people who say it is hard to confess their sins?

IVAN: I think it is because their faith is weak. You can feel Our Lady's presence in Medjugorje. Many young people seek the passing things in life and forget about God.

FR SLAVKO: What does Confession mean to you?

IVAN: For me it is a cleansing and a liberating from those things which I know are mistakes. In other words, it means, for one thing, an unburdening of my problems.

FR SLAVKO: What can you say to young people who are ashamed or afraid to show their faith?

IVAN: In modern society young people are afraid to say that. We ought to develop our faith and give an example to others on how to live our faith.

FR SLAVKO: Did you ever feel ashamed to tell others that you believe in God?

IVAN: Yes, before the apparition I sometimes felt ashamed. But now while the apparitions are going on, I cannot on the one hand continue looking at Our Lady and on the other hide my faith from people.

FR SLAVKO: How does one pray with the heart?

IVAN: For me you pray with the heart when you desire to pray, when you absorb every word you pray. Besides that you must be relaxed. That prayer brings joy, happiness and strength for life. Vocal prayer does not give that kind of joy in families. We ought to train in the practice of prayer with the heart. We cannot pray with our heart just by praying with our mouths.

FR SLAVKO: Can you explain the joy of that prayer?

IVAN: It is easy. I do it by reading the Bible. It is a spontaneous prayer which means much to me. I cannot pray amid the confusion of the day. The best time for me is evening time. Spontaneous prayer means a lot to me.

FR SLAVKO: Sometimes young people feel unhappy, deserted by God. They think that Our Lady and Jesus do not understand them. What do you say?

IVAN: Our Lady does not desert anybody. She loves everyone of us. It is just our opinion that She has deserted us. Maybe some of us are deserted by our families, or we have deserted them, and that is the source of our unhappiness.

FR SLAVKO: Can you advise readers how to follow the way of Jesus and Mary?

IVAN: Priests should refer constantly to the Gospels. They should speak simply, so that they can be understood. Secondly, the families ought to apply everything that our Church teaches.

FR SLAVKO: What did Mary mean when She said we ought to be strong in our faith, especially the young?

IVAN: In many of Her messages, Our Lady has stressed the importance of strong faith. The only things which life can offer us are passing things. People easily oscillate and, in varying between extremes, can fall down totally. Then they are disappointed and cannot put their beliefs in prospective. Our Lady said we ought to pray, so that through prayer our faith will gain strength.

FR SLAVKO: Tell us something of your prayer group?

IVAN: The subject of prayer groups is a very big one and there is much that could be said about it. I can start with my own prayer group: my prayer group was formed in 1982. Even the forming of that group was spontaneous. We were sitting together one night talking and we made a plan to form a group. After that we suggested it to Our Lady that we wanted this. Our Lady accepted this plan with joy, and the group was formed. We started getting together step by step. During the three months we used to meet on our own. After three months Our Lady approved and expressed a wish to come with us. There were sixteen members of different ages, married couples, young and old but mainly young. The aim of the group is definitely a big one, like assisting Our Lady in carrying out Her plans. The second thing is that we are growing spiritually, living Her messages, praying, doing penance. Again, the second thing is to live with Our Lady. Simply living Her messages means to live with Her, because all the messages which She gives to my group – i.e. our group – are messages which lead us on the right way to Heaven.

Some of our forgetfulness is tolerated but it cannot always be tolerated. Everybody has a right to forgetfulness but the group should be living each message and the messages should be brought together. It is not possible for us to accept that any member of the group lives one message without living the rest of them, because they are all linked together and must all be lived, so that that person will grow spiritually, in the proper way. We are meeting on Mondays and Fridays and our meetings consist of singing, praying, reading the bible and meditating together.

Our meetings exist even outside the group when we are talking together at other times, discussing our problems and difficulties regarding the group. That's when we are sorting them out.

Just like each person, each group has its highs and lows, but each one should sense when he is down and when he is vulnerable. The worst can happen when a man knows he is down, and he does not know how to get up, nor does he have the formula for getting up. The person who leads the group is very important. The group needs to have the right leader to point each one in the right direction and lead them on the right way. In this case, the leader of the group … in this, my case, the leader of the group is Our Lady Herself.

Forming Groups
Talking about forming groups today. I think that question is very difficult and very detailed. We have to know that each forming of a group and each one who wants to form a group should know what to do and what

the aims of that group are, and what that group intends to do. Each group should have its leader, and each leader should know how to lead the group. Today many who are forming groups try too hard at the beginning – they form a group and at the start just try too hard. It is not the right way. It should not be done that way. In the beginning we need to work with a group slowly and step by step. Later on when we see the group is coming together as one unit then we can look for better results. But I am saying you need to have patience with a group.

Priests and Lay People
Something else I could point out regarding the groups. In the last few messages Our Lady Herself stressed that priests should form the groups in their own parishes and lay people also, if they are spiritually sound and mature. She brings to our attention that young people in today's world are in a difficult position. Priests should influence young people and bring them together in these groups where they would lead them along the way of goodness, happiness and joy – the way to a real and a happy life.

As I already mentioned, each group consists of young people and this is the way it should be. I do not exclude the older, but young people today are in a difficult situation, and prayer groups are the right way for them to be helped in a spiritual way.

Our Lady is specially bringing to our attention that She wants young people to come together and that She wants us to follow the way of goodness.

I have already mentioned that young people today are in a very difficult position, and in our age the world needs to give a little more attention and a little bit more time to young people, and I am saying this especially for the parents. We all know that the question of youth is an urgent one. We are all aware. We all know the effects of alcohol and drugs and young people are accepting that as a good thing. On the contrary, this is not good. These bring sorrow and sadness. Death, sorrow and sadness affects parents most. Why had parents not looked at this problem before.

In my opinion they approached the problem wrongly. Firstly, they did not devote to their children time or love. Neither did they pray with them, talk to, or help their children with their problems. They have not been open to their children so their children were not open with them. Maybe the parents themselves were not reared properly, so therefore they could not show the right way. The reason may be that parents were not in agreement with each other. If parents do not agree then they cannot direct properly.

Nowadays the world has a lot to offer young people. We all know that. But what it has to offer is only temporal. Whatever God and Our Lady have to offer is the food of which man must feed himself. That's real spiritual food. I do not mean that we must not accept anything from the world. What I am saying is that we must limit what we take from the world. Much of what the world has to offer can lead us on the wrong way, mislead us. I am saying, cooperation between parents and children must be mutual. This is important.

Once again, about the group: each group which is working well, praying well will surely go the right way. Prayers, according to Our Lady should be with the heart and not the lips.

FR SLAVKO: What does it mean to pray with the heart?

IVAN: To pray with the heart means that each word we say, we should think about and absorb, so that each word can strengthen us, give us new strength, relax us and make us happy. To pray with the lips means to say words without meaning.

All the messages which Our Lady is giving us, messages of peace, conversion, prayer and penance means everything in life to us and man needs to live them. The groups themselves live Our Lady's messages, messages of peace, prayer, conversion and penance.

We cannot spread peace to other people if we do not have that peace ourselves. The fact must be clear to us. Neither can we pray if we do not have peace in ourselves.

Regarding penance, Our Lady brought to our attention that on Wednesdays and Fridays we should fast on bread and water and apart from that we should give up particular things which we like. What do we get from penance? From penance we get purification from the things which are affecting us. We are fighting against Satan, because recently Our Lady stressed that he is very powerful, especially with young people. If young people do not try hard enough they will be overcome. She is inviting us to pray for young people all over the world.

The formation of prayer groups is definitely Our Lady's wish and they are, for sure, the fruits of Medjugorje. Each member who joins a group on the basis of Medjugorje, and on the basis of the messages, comes back to real life. That's a fruit ... those are Our Lady's messages and according to them he converts himself. He changes his life. By joining a group a man is improving himself and changing himself.

FR SLAVKO: Ivan, will you promise that you will recommend all the readers of this conversation to Our Lady?

IVAN: I want to reassure all the young people of the world that they are in my prayers, and I will certainly recommend them to Our Lady so that we will work together for the future. Today's world offers a great deal to young people. Parents, too, give a lot to their children, but perhaps they give them too much freedom. The future gives ground for hope, and I hope that young people justify that hope. I hope that young people reading this will pray for the visionaries, because they need prayers too. Let us pray for each other, let our prayer bind us together, so that we grow up together with prayer. Let us develop by prayer and through prayer find peace, because if there is no peace in our hearts, there is no peace in our families, and in the world.

The visionary Ivan with his wife Maureen and baby daughter pictured on their way to evening devotions.

Priests on Retreat

For several years now, groups of priests from areas as diverse as Europe to South America and quite often accompanied by their Bishop have been making the pilgrimage to Medjugorje for the purpose of spiritual retreat and renewal of their vows.

While addressing one such group of a hundred and twenty priests, Fr Tomislav, speaking on the theme 'In the Eucharist, God offers everything', was asked a most important question regarding the goal or what the essence of a prayer group should be:

> If we understood the liturgical journey with the Mass, God's people would go far. If we priests, celebrating the Mass – living the Eucharist – were to follow the steps of the liturgy, we could lead the people towards permanent, continual prayer. Our Eucharist will be a spiritual catechism, a true journey of the parish, at least for those who go ahead. I have seen very few priests who live this liturgical journey.
>
> Let's reflect a little on last week (31st Ordinary Time). The Psalmist prays at the beginning: 'Hurry, Lord.' And in the Gospel Jesus says: 'Hurry, Zacchaus.' I pray and He says 'Hurry, come.' In this week there is a step by step call. Monday's call,

opening the door to the poor people, to those who disliked, who are not [our] friends, those to invite to the banquet (Luke 14:12–14). What does opening mean in the spiritual sense? What does it mean when I find many people who are my enemies in my heart? I have to live this healing within myself and have to lead the people to this healing.

Only those who have totally offered themselves enter into the Lord's banquet (Luke 14:15–24). We have to be ready, spiritually open – seeing that one day you prepare for the next – they are continual steps. Today, the Lord will call us (Luke 14:25–33) to leave everything, even one's own life, and sow only love within ourselves. We have no other duty, says St Paul to the Romans (13:8–10) than to love one another. If we priests live this life-transformation through the Eucharist, if we live our spirituality, then this becomes easy. All the rest continues this Eucharist – as Our Lady has said, 'Live the Eucharist every day.' If our Eucharist were this liturgical journey, then Christians who follow the Mass would advance along the spiritual path. I believe that our churches would be full. There would be more people, that's for sure: I see how starved people are.

The Fruit of the Eucharist

And what of the fruits of the Eucharist? What is the blessing at the end of the Eucharist? I think that the majority of priests have a king's attitude towards the leper: What can I do for you, sick person? What have I for you who are afflicted? I don't have the time! No! We have to understand first of all that before entering into the Eucharist we have to present all the sufferings of souls, we have to give to the Lord all the sufferings of the parish, of the sick: we have to bring all these within ourselves. A key message was given to the prayer group: 'Many pray, but never enter into prayer.' The steps to follow were explained: renounce and give all problems to the Lord, give all sins to the Lord, and when we feel we have handed all our problems and all our sins to Him, then we can enter into the life of prayer.

You see, if we approach the Eucharist having prepared ourselves beforehand, bring with us everything within ourselves; and if we totally openly welcome the grace of God who transforms us after the Eucharist, then there must be fruit. What happened to the prophet Elisha and to Naaman will also happen. If we enter into the Eucharist we could experience all the graces which the Lord has promised us.

I would like to conclude by saying that we priests really have to live the Eucharist to derive that joy of the resurrection, the power of God who offers Himself for the salvation of the world. This cannot happen in our life if we make a ritual instead of the Eucharist, if we do not permit this process within ourselves. On the contrary, the Eucharist will really be a transformation of the people, parish, group, community, and, in this way, through the liturgical journey, we can advance all the time in depth, experiencing more and more the joy and almightiness of God. At that time we will have something to give to the people if we permit God to live in us; at that time He can act; He will not find obstacles in manifesting His face and giving fruits to us and to the people.

Fr Tomislav in Conversation with the Priests

Question: How can prayer groups be led on this liturgical journey?

Every group has to be led towards the Eucharist, otherwise it will not work. It is necessary to bring the group to the Eucharist, otherwise the groups will close up within themselves and will not have that ecclesiastical strength which comes from the Eucharist.

In the history of the Church we know of many movements which were closed up within themselves and how there was war between these movements. This does not happen if we live the Eucharist – brotherhood, openness. The priest, as minister of the local church, has to bring these groups to the centre, which offers the depth and width of the Church. Then the groups will become stable.

I also believe that there are other movements to be looked at. All groups should advance and mature, and they should receive stability and commitment from the Church through brotherhood (as laid down in the new Constitution of the Franciscan Third Order). In this way, the more spiritually mature person can be much more committed in the parish. They can be chosen by the parish priest to direct groups in order to bring together these groups in the Eucharist, in one Spirit. Also, people go where there is more offered. Sometimes not enough is offered in the parishes, or the priests are not committed enough, or there are no provisions for a more profound journey. It is necessary that we priests earn, and permit, this depth in our parishes. We need to evaluate what we are doing and act accordingly. I believe that as a priest, above all, I must live the Eucharist.

Question: Can we priests live the Eucharist without giving a little time to private adoration every day?
I don't think so, because if we live the Eucharist deeply, that communication with God which I have spoken about should continue in our work throughout the day. But we cannot do this without having contact with the Eucharistic Jesus. My experience, these last years, is that just there, in front of the Most Holy Sacrament, the Eucharist revives me, and when in adoration of the Most Holy Sacrament I receive major graces.

Question: Would you say something on the group experience that you have had which the visionary Marija participated in?
It is the experience of going right to the bottom of the Eucharist in the transformation of the person. Those who want to live this consecration, live this offering for their brothers, giving their own life to others. And here we have

arrived to what the Eucharist means. Often we have heard of people who have offered themselves as victims, and we might feel negative towards this. But it is a positive thing.

Steps exist to come down from Heaven to earth and to climb up from earth to Heaven. Jesus humiliated Himself, offering Himself completely. Our Lady followed this path of humility, making a total offering of self, and thus reaching Heaven. Souls which offer themselves completely to God become completely transformed inwardly. That experience is a call when people leave everything and spend their lives in prayer, in adoration, in brotherly love, and become participants in the Eucharist so that in a community the Eucharist becomes the centre as sacrament and, at the same time, the journey of a group [community] in order to be offered completely.

Our Lady as a Guide

From time to time we have been allowed to gleam some, but only some, of the cherished words and guidance of the Mother of God to the prayer group, as given through Jelena and Marijana. Jelena assures me that she has carefully recorded each encounter and that when Our Lady permits it, all will be made known to us.

Meantime, we give here, some very beautiful and spiritually enriching reflections by Fr Tomislav and Fr Slavko on

certain, but individual messages to the group. These messages of guidance on the road to sanctification are additional to, but forming part of the (150) weekly and (still continuing) monthly messages being given by Our Lady to the parish of Medjugorje and the whole world.

For reasons of sheer volume, these reflections on Our Lady's words have had to be abbreviated here, but are available elsewhere in their full text.

The Messages

Our Lady's main messages are those of *peace, prayer, fasting, the sacraments and urgent conversion.*

At the beginning, Our Lady presented herself saying:

❦   I am the Queen of Peace.

And so, the first message that She sent to the world is one of peace. This message is the essential one around which all else revolves. The context of this message is this: 'The world with all its present tensions is going towards its ruin. If it wants to be saved, it must have peace, but it will only have peace if it finds God, those who find God find a joy in their hearts from which comes peace.'

Here is the second message which has been repeated to us a thousand times:

❦   Be converted, be converted, be converted.

Then come the messages of prayer and fasting. Our Lady says:

❦   There are many Christians who no longer believe because they do not pray. So start with at least seven Our Fathers, Hail Marys, Glory

Bes and the Creed every day. Fast on Fridays on bread and water. Fasting cannot be substituted by prayer and almsgiving; only the sick can substitute it by prayer and almsgiving.

Then She stressed the need for monthly confession and for a full participation in the Holy Eucharist. Once She spoke of the Holy Eucharist saying:

⚜ Those Christians who go to church without preparation, without receiving Holy Communion, without giving thanks, it is better that they do not go because their hearts become hard.

She said to Jelena:

⚜ When you go to church, start preparing for Mass as soon as you leave home and never leave the church without thanking God.

Sacraments and an Urgent Conversion

Through Jelena, Our Lady expressed the wish several times that the world be consecrated to the Heart of Jesus and to the Immaculate Heart. In the Autumn She emphasised this and dictated two prayers of consecration.

In the last week of Advent, Our Lady said:

⚜ Start invoking the Holy Spirit every day in church.

Later on She recommended that the invocation to the Holy Spirit be made, not only in church, but also in the family. The subject of prayer to the Holy Spirit is greatly stressed by Our Lady. Once She said:

Many people pray in the wrong way, they ask for graces, but few ask for the grace of the Holy Spirit. But it is those who receive the gift of the Holy Spirit who have received everything. First of all, ask for the gift of the Holy Spirit.

Before Mass it is necessary to pray to the Holy Spirit.

In November 1983 through Jelena Our Lady told the group:

I am your mother full of goodness and Jesus is your great friend. Do not fear anything in His presence. Give Him your heart. From the bottom of your heart tell Him your sufferings, thus you will be invigorated in prayer, with a free heart, in a peace without fear.

In December She thanked the group:

Thanks to all of you who have come here, so numerous during this year, in spite of snow, ice, and bad weather, to pray to Jesus. Continue, hold on in your suffering. You know well that when a friend asks you for something you give it to him. It is thus with Jesus. When you pray without ceasing and you come in spite of your tiredness, He will give you all that you ask from Him. For that, pray.

On the evening before the Feast of the Immaculate Conception She told the group:

Tomorrow will really be a blessed day for you, if every moment is consecrated to my Immaculate

Heart. Abandon yourselves to me. Strive to have your joy grow, to live in the faith, to change your hearts.

Early Messages to the Prayer Group through Jelena
January 1984
In the weeks before Christmas, Our Lady had asked for prayers for the outpouring of the Holy Spirit. In the New Year the group thought they could stop saying the prayer to the Holy Spirit, thinking Our Lady only wanted it said until Christmas. So She said:

✿ Why have you stopped saying the prayer to the Holy Spirit? I have asked you to pray always and at all times so that the Holy Spirit may descend over all of you. Begin again to pray for that.

✿ My children, pray; I say it again, pray! Know that in your life the most important thing is prayer.

✿ Before all, pray; I say it again, pray! Know that in your life the most important thing is prayer.

✿ My children, pray! I say it again, pray! I will say it to you again. Do not think that Jesus is going to manifest Himself again in the manger; friends, He is born again in your hearts.

✿ I know that I speak to you very often about prayer; but know that there are many people in the world who do not pray, who do not even know what to say in prayer.

✑ Pray and fast! I wish that in your hearts prayer and fasting flourish.'

✑ I wish to engrave in every heart the sign of love. If you love all mankind, then there is peace in you. If you are at peace with all men, it is the kingdom of love.

✑ Pray and fast, because without prayer you cannot do anything.

✑ Pray and fast. Do not give up on meditation. At home meditate at least half an hour.

✑ Pray and fast. You have to understand well what it means to pray. May you understand that; I desire it very much.

✑ Pray and fast. You need vigour in your prayer. May you be in recollection for a long time and fervently.

✑ Thank you for adoring my Son in the Sacred Host. That touches me very much. As for you, pray! I desire to see you happy.

✑ Pray and fast. I wish that you always deepen your life in prayer. Every morning say the Prayer of Consecration to the Heart of Mary. Do it in family. Recite each morning the Angelus (once), The Lord's Prayer, the Hail Mary and the Glory Be five times in honour of the Holy Passion, and a sixth time for our Holy Father, the Pope. Then say the Creed and the Prayer to the Holy Spirit; and, if it is possible, it would be well to pray one part of the rosary.

❧   I wish that all of you pray, and that my heart extends to the whole world. I wish to be with you.

❧   Pray and fast! I wish for you to purify your hearts. Purify them and open them to me.

❧   Pray! I desire to purify your hearts. Pray. It is indispensable, because God gives you the greatest graces when you pray.

❧   Pray! Do not think of anything, pray. Do not think of anything else except of those for whom you pray. Then prayer will be better and you will be faithful to it.

❧   Continue to help the poor, the sick, and to pray for the dead. You should not feel any fear. Let all free themselves completely and let them abandon their hearts to me so that I can be with them. Have them listen to me and discover me in the poor, and in every man.

February 1984

❧   It is raining at this time, and you say: 'It is not reasonable to go to church in this slush. Why is it raining so much?' Do not ever speak like that. You have not ceased to pray so that God may send you rain which makes the earth rich, then do not turn against this blessing from God. Above all, thank Him through prayer and fasting.

✿ Pray, because I need more prayers. Be reconciled, because I desire reconciliation among you and more love for each other, like brothers. I wish that prayer, peace and love bloom in you.

✿ Pray, because prayer is very necessary to you. With prayer, your body and soul will find peace. One must be pious and set a good example for others, in order to awaken in them the faith. It is necessary to pray as much as possible while offering your heart. One has to consecrate himself if he wants to be truly better.

✿ Pray and fast. I desire to live in your hearts.

✿ Some of them still have a week of rest. They do not fast … others have come here and fast on Wednesday, Thursday and Friday. Others help the poor and the sick. Others love everybody and want to discover Jesus in each one. Some are not convinced, others are. Those are mine. See how they honour me. Lead them to me so that I may bless them.

✿ Pray, pray, I ask of you.

✿ From you, I expect only prayer. Thus pray.

□ Pray, pray! How many persons have followed other beliefs or sectors and have abandoned Jesus Christ! They create their own gods; they adore idols. How that hurts me! If they could be converted! How unbelievers are in large numbers! That will change only if you help me with your prayers.

□ Pray and fast! I desire humility from you; but you can become humble only through prayer and fasting.

□ Open your hearts to me, I desire to bless them fully.

□ I ask of you to pray and fast! Pray for the peace and humility of your hearts.

□ Fast and pray! Give me your hearts. I desire to change them completely. I desire for them to be pure.

□ Pray and fast! I desire you to purify your hearts completely. I wish to make you happy.

Our Lady referred to a very strong, icy wind blowing which everyone noticed on the way to church:

□ The wind is my sign. I will come in the wind. When the wind blows know that I am with you. You have learned that the cross represents Christ; it is a sign of Him. It is the same for the crucifix you have in your home. For me, it is not the same. When it is cold, you come to church;

you want to offer everything to God. I am, then, with you. I am with you in the wind. Do not be afraid.

❧ My children, pray! The world has been drawn into a great whirlpool. It does not know what it is doing. It does not realise in what sin it is sinking. It needs your prayers so that I can pull it out of this danger.

❧ Pray and fast! I desire to purify you and to save you. For that, help me with your prayers.

❧ Pray and fast! I expect generosity and prayer from your hearts.

❧ I hold all of you in my arms. You are mine. I need your prayers so that you may all be mine. I desire to be all yours and for you to be all mine. I receive all your prayers. I receive them with joy.

❧ Pray and fast! I desire to be with you always. I desire to stay in your hearts always and for you to stay in mine.

❧ Know that I love all of you. Know that you are all mine. To no one do I desire to give more than to you. Come to me all of you. Stay with me. I want to be your mother. Come, I desire all of you.

❧ Pray and fast! Know that I love you. I hold all of you on my knees.

❋   Do not be tired. I desire to be with you.

❋   Pray and fast! Love everyone on earth, just as you love yourselves.

❋   Have each one decide alone. In the meantime it would be good that this week they fast on Thursday. Have them read the Bible and meditate on it.

❋   Pray! It may seem strange to you that I always speak of prayer, and yet I say: pray! Why do you hesitate? In Holy Scripture you have heard it said, 'Do not worry about tomorrow, each day will have its own worries.' Then do not worry about the other days. Be content with prayer. Your mother will take care of the rest.

March 1984

To Mirjana:

❋   Pray and fast. When I tell you to pray, do not think that you have to pray more but pray. Let prayer and faith awaken in your hearts.

❋   Each Thursday, read again the passages of Matthew 6:24–34, before the Most Blessed Sacrament, or if it is not possible to come to church, do it with your family.

❋   Pray and fast! Ask the Holy Spirit to renew your souls, to renew the entire world.

In preparation for the feast of the Annunciation:

✤ Pray and fast, so that during this novena, God will fill you with His Power.

✤ Today I rejoice with all my angels. The first part of my program has been achieved.

Our Lady crying:

✤ There are so many men who live in sin. Here there are likewise among you some people who have offended my heart. Pray and fast for them.

✤ Yesterday evening I said that the first part of my plan was realised.

✤ In the group, some have given themselves up to God so that He may guide them. Allow the will of God be realised in you.

✤ My children, I wish that the Holy Mass be for you the gift of the day. Attend it, wish for it to begin. Jesus gives Himself to you during the Mass. Thus, look forward to that moment when you are cleansed. Pray very much so that the Holy Spirit will renew your parish. If people attend Mass with lukewarmness, they will return to their homes cold and with an empty heart.

April 1984

❦   I ask for you to pray for the conversion of all men. For that, I need your prayers.

❦   How can you not be happy? Jesus gives Himself to you. I wish to inundate souls. If I am sad this evening, the reason is that many have not prepared themselves for Easter. They do not permit Jesus on that day to unite Himself to their souls.

Holy Week

❦   Raise your hands and open your hearts. Now at the time of the Resurrection, Jesus wishes to give you a special gift. This gift of my Son is my gift. Here it is. You will be subjected to trials and you will endure them with great ease. We will be ready to show you how to escape from them if you accept us. Do not say that the Holy Year has ended and that there is no need to pray. On the contrary, double your prayers because the Holy Year is just another step ahead.

The Risen Jesus, with rays of light coming forth from His wounds, appeared and said:

❦   Receive my graces and tell the whole world that there is no happiness except through me.

Jelena asked Our Lady this question for Father Vlasic: 'How could Jesus pray all night? With what method?'
Our Lady said:

- He had a great longing for God and for the salvation of souls.

- You should be filled with joy. Today Jesus died for your salvation.

*The thirty-five foot cross on the mountain overlooking Medjugorje.
Our Lady, in the early days of the apparitions, was seen by
many thousands of people praying here. She confirmed to the
visionaries by saying she is always in adoration at
three o'clock, the hour of Divine Mercy.*

Prayer to the Mother of Goodness, Love and Mercy

O Mother mine,
Mother of goodness, love and mercy,
I love You infinitely
and I offer myself to You.
By means of Your goodness, Your love,
and Your grace, save me.
I desire to be yours.
I love You infinitely,
and desire You to protect me.
From the depth of my heart I pray You,
Mother of goodness,
give me Your goodness.
Let me gain Heaven by means of it.
I pray you, by Your infinite love,
to give me the grace,
so that I may love every man,
as You have loved Jesus Christ.
I pray You to give me the grace
to be merciful towards You.
I offer myself to You completely and desire
that You follow my ever step.
Because you are full of grace.
And I desire that I will never forget this.
And if, by chance, I should lose grace,
I pray you to restore it to me once more.
Amen.

This beautiful prayer was given by Our Lady to Jelena Vasilj, 19 April 1983. The phrase 'I pray you to give me the grace to be merciful towards you' means 'Give me the grace to love your will which is different to mine'.

✎ He descends into Hell and opens the gates of paradise. Let joy reign in your hearts.

✎ When you pray, pray more. Prayer is a conversation with God. To pray means to listen to the Lord. Prayer is for me a service, because after it, all things become clear. Prayer leads to knowing happiness.

✎ Raise your hands, yearn for Jesus because in His Resurrection, He wants to fill you with graces. Be enthusiastic about the Resurrection. All of us in Heaven are happy, but we seek the joy of your hearts. My Son's gift and mine, at this moment is this: you will be comforted in your trials, they will be easier for you because we will be close to you. If you listen to us, we will show you how to overcome them.

✎ Pray much tomorrow. May Jesus truly rise in your families. Where there is war, may peace come. I wish that a new man would be born in your hearts. My children, I thank you. Continue to bring about the Resurrection of Jesus in all men. The Holy Year has ended, but it represents only a step in our life. Continue to pray.

✎ Many times, confronting justice and confronting your sins, many times I returned from your home in tears. I could not say a single word. I am your mother and I do not want to oppose you. But what I shall do in you is up to you.

✎ We must rejoice in Jesus, to make Him happy.

May

❧ Dear children, at this time it is especially necessary for you to consecrate yourselves to me and to my heart. Love, pray and fast.

❧ O dear children, how I wish that you would turn to me. See, my little children, it is the end of the school year and you have not even reached halfway. That is why now you must become a little more serious.

❧ I wish that the parish prepare itself through a novena, to receive the sacrament of Confirmation on the day of the feast of the Ascension.

❧ I truly wish that you would be pure on the day of Pentecost. Pray, pray that your spirit be changed on that day.

❧ Dear children, thank you for every prayer. Try to pray continuously, and do not forget that I love you and wish that all of you would love one another.

In answer to questions Jelena was requested to ask Our Lady:

❧ For all of these questions, there is an answer: pray to the Holy Spirit, so that He may enlighten you, and you will come to know all that you wish.

❧ Love is a gift from God. Therefore, pray that God may give you the gift of love.

The priests should visit families, more particularly those who do not practise anymore, and who have forgotten God. Priests should carry the Gospel of Jesus to the people, and teach them how to pray. And the priests themselves should pray more and also fast. They should give to the poor what they don't need.

Regarding the celebration of Our Lady's two-thousandth birthday:

Throughout the centuries, I have given myself to you. Is it too much to give me three days? Do not work on those days. Take your rosaries and pray. Fasting has been forgotten during the last quarter of the century within the Catholic Church.

Jelena tells Our Lady that if She tells the people to pray four hours a day they will back out:

Don't you understand, that is only one-sixth of the day?

May the love of God be always with you, because without it, you cannot be fully converted. Let the rosary in your hands make you think of Jesus.

Dear children, strive to penetrate into the Mass, just as you should.

Thank you for every prayer. Continue to pray, but pray with the heart. Dear children, again it is necessary for you to pray to the Holy Spirit and it would be good for you to pray the Lord's Prayer seven times in the church, as one does it for Pentecost.

During the Pentecost Novena, before each Our Father, the priest asks for one of the seven gifts of the Holy Spirit:

⁂ Dear children, I am happy that you have begun to pray as I requested of you. Continue.

⁂ Dear children, you need love, I have said it to you many times, and I remind you. Continue only to pray and be happy because I am with you.

⁂ I wish that you continue to pray and to fast.

⁂ I wish that you would become like a flower in the spring. The love which I give you is great, but sometimes you reject it, and thus, it becomes less. Always accept immediately the gifts which I give you so that you can profit from them.

⁂ Prepare yourselves through prayer for the third anniversary of the beginning of the apparitions. June 25th should be celebrated as the Feast of Mary, 'Queen of Peace'.

⁂ If you knew how much I love you, you would cry with joy. When anyone is before you and asks you something, you will give it to him.

✤ I am before so many hearts, but they remain closed. Pray so that the world receives my love.

✤ Each member of the group is like a flower; and if someone tries to crush you, you will grow and will try to grow even more. If someone crushes you a little, you will recover. And if someone pulls a petal, continue to grow as though you were complete.

To Mirjana:

✤ My only wish is that you become as joyful and enthusiastic as you were during the first days of my apparitions.

✤ Dear children, I am very happy that there are so many people here this evening. Thank God alone.

Holy Week 1984
Our Lady gave some very special messages through Jelena for the prayer group during Holy Week. Messages of singular significance:

For Good Friday She said:

✤ You must be very happy. Today Jesus died for your salvation. He descended into Hell, opened the doors of Paradise and opened the door of Paradise into your hearts; so you must be happy.

Fr Tomislav tells us how surprised he was: 'I was surprised that Our Lady was not weeping and calling us to penance, but actually on Good Friday said: "You must be very happy."'

For Holy Saturday, Our Lady said:

✤ Prepare yourselves in a special way for Holy Saturday; do not ask me why for Saturday, but I repeat to you: prepare yourselves for Holy Saturday.

For Easter Sunday Our Lady gave a very beautiful and moving meditation. Jelena relates it as follows:

✤ Lift up your hands, long for Jesus because at this time of His Resurrection He wishes to give you graces. I am telling everyone to be enthusiastic about the Resurrection of Jesus. Meditate, meditate on this. Heaven and earth are praising Him because He is risen.

Then, after a silence, She said:

✤ All of us in Heaven are happy but we need joy in your hearts. My gift and that of my Son Jesus, which we are offering to you now, is this: your ordeals will be lightened. We will be close to you in your difficulties and will show you the way out of them if you accept Us. I am, doing my best to translate this for you; to continue: Now in moments of trial you will be especially helped and the trials made easier for you.

Then She added:

✦ Pray a great deal, pray tomorrow that Jesus is truly risen, so that He may be truly risen in your families. There is much quarrelling and I want to transform it into resurrection and peace. I want something to be born in your hearts. Do not say that the Year of Redemption is over and you do not need to pray but rather strengthen your prayer. May the Year of Redemption be only a stepping stone in your lives.

Jelena has seen the Risen Jesus and a brilliant light shining from His wounds. Jesus blesses everyone, telling them to continuously experience the graces and joys in their hearts and to tell everyone in the world that salvation comes from Him and Him alone. At the end Our Lady said:

✦ My children, thank you! Continue reawakening the Resurrection of Jesus in all men.

Mirjana then added that Our Lady also said:

✦ Dear children, today I am joyful because many of the faithful have truly lived Holy Saturday as I desired.

No Guidelines

Our Lady is guiding the prayer group on an interior level. Fr Tomislav explains:

> It is useless for people wanting to organise prayer groups to come to us for guidelines because Our Lady does not speak of guidelines here, but guides in an interior way. We can offer the group leaders our experiences along the pilgrimage with Our Lady, but I say at once to those who wish to organise prayer groups: consecrate yourselves totally to Our Lady and I guarantee that She will be in your midst and will guide you in an interior way. A woman from Milan asked Our Lady through Jelena: 'Dear Mother, as you see we have come from Milan to visit you, when are you coming to Milan to visit us?' Our Lady replied: 'When you open your hearts to me.' This is the answer to all those who are seeking Our Lady and wish to follow this road. Our Lady is truly present wherever there is a true opening of heart and guides every group and person. This is why it is useless to ask for guidelines because, as I have seen with this prayer group, Our Lady has a definite purpose.

False Prophecies and True Prophecies

I have to explain several things to you so that you are able to walk truly on the path of spiritual life. Some people come to Medjugorje and immediately, when they hear that these apparitions will be the last ones of Our Lady on earth and hear about the secrets, they become frightened and start saying that soon there will be a catastrophe, soon there will be a war, soon troubles will come. As to this Our Lady said:

> Those who say that on such a day, in such a year, there will be a catastrophe are all also prophets. I have always said: be converted, be converted. Your future depends on your conversion.

It is from this that we are able to see the difference between true and false prophecies. That is, false prophecies are always fantastic, whilst the Biblical prophecies are always conditional: If Nineveh had converted, it would not have been destroyed. As you see, it depends on us and, for this reason, Our Lady always stresses the messages of peace, prayer and fasting.

Peace is a Positive, Inner Attitude

Through Jelena, Our Lady said:

> Love is peace, peace is love.

When we speak of peace here you must understand it as a deeper spiritual reality, an attitude, a profound gift from which all others originate. Jelena explains this attitude of peace by saying: 'Our Lady does not like speaking of sin but, when She has to do so, She seems to be weeping because from the very beginning of Her life She has always lived a pure life without sin.' This is why Our Lady says:

> Do not think of wars, punishment, evil, because
> if you do so you are on the road towards them.
> Your task is to accept the divine peace, to live it
> and to spread it.

From this we can see what is meant by peace: it is a totally positive attitude. Now you can understand that passage of the Gospel of St Matthew 6:23–34, when Our Lady calls for a total abandonment at every level, because in this way you can arrive at the true peace She desires. When Our Lady says 'Be converted' you must take a step forward. The majority of people who come to Medjugorje for the first time remain on a superficial level, asking for healing, solving of marital problems, for their children, for the solution to various problems, but always on an earthly level. Divine peace cannot be found on this level we are still in the condition of bearing our fears in our heart. This is why there are fears for the future and fanatical Christians who frighten others saying that Our Lady is menacing and so on. To solve this problem we must look realistically at our lives and at the true Christian life.

Fear does not Exist for the Christian

I know for sure that soon I will undergo a catastrophe: in a few months time, in a few years, in hospital, at home, on the road or by an atom bomb, the effect is the same for me: I will die. This is my catastrophe. The only catastrophe of my earthly life. I believe that you, too, are certain of undergoing this catastrophe. If we shut our eyes and pretend death does not exist for us, we are deceiving ourselves and we will try to protect ourselves, to save ourselves from this catastrophe. Instead, we Christians will not undergo a catastrophe because, for us, life consists primarily in eternal life. This life is only a transition. I say this in a very special way after the experiences I have had here because, in a certain sense, through the visionaries, we have been able to touch Heaven, Paradise, because they have all seen Paradise. Three of them have had the experience of being taken up to Heaven. If we truly accept eternal life, a catastrophe does not exist for us any longer. This life is only a transition. We must truly accept this essentially Christian fact and then all fear will vanish, there will be no more fear of the future and we will be capable of accepting divine peace, of living it and spreading it as Our Lady tells us. Otherwise, we cannot be true messengers when we speak of peace and the apparitions of Medjugorje. We will talk of punishment, troubles, secrets and we will spread fear. Our Lady has repeated several times:

> Your task is to receive divine peace, to live it
> and to spread it.

Open your Hearts and Obtain Graces

I must explain something else to those who come here to ask for the grace of healing and so on. Our Lady always replied to everyone:

> The most important thing is to believe, to have faith, to pray every day for the same intention, to fast on Fridays on bread and water. For the gravely sick, pray more and fast more.

When Our Lady says that the priority is to have faith, this does not only mean to believe that God exists. The faith of which Our Lady speaks here is an opening of one's whole self to God, in a total abandonment to Him. We can be helped to understand this if we read the episode in the Gospel of St John, Chapter 4, where Jesus meets the Samaritan woman. They started to talk about water and Jesus entered into her heart and found evil there because she had been married six times, she was an adulteress. An opening of heart had come about. Jesus wants to walk with us, so all of you, if you have a special intention you must set out on the path of faith. Perhaps you will not obtain it in five days, maybe five months will be necessary. Some intentions will be granted already today, but it is necessary to set out. With regard to advice that you often ask for here, I would say this: start out in faith with your priests and group leaders. Later, along the way, Jesus will draw near and will make it clear to us, deep down, what we have to do.

Let yourselves be Guided by God

I believe that the most important messages for our spiritual life were given in Medjugorje. The essential one given by Our Lady is this:

> If you want to be very happy, live a simple, humble life, pray a great deal, do not delve into your problems, but let yourselves be guided by God.

I have meditated for many days on this message and I see it as a fundamental, because our problems are the result of a really complicated life, which we have complicated with various philosophies and so on. Our Lady, on the contrary, leads us to a sincere and simple life. Several times during this period She has repeated to me, through a visionary:

> Do not complicate matters. Yes, you can walk on a deeper spiritual way into your problems but let yourselves be guided by Jesus Christ.

Most people who go deeply into their problems, aggravate matters and block Jesus and His work for us. On the other hand, putting ourselves in the hands of God with simplicity means leaving room for Him, who is Master of our Life and of all the mysteries. I see a great sin in the world in this: we have taken over many areas of our lives that should only belong to Jesus Christ.

Have a Great Desire for God

About the method of prayer, Our Lady said this:

> The fundamental point about prayer is to have a great desire for God and for the salvation of man. If you possess these desires then you will pray and find time for prayer.

Our Lady always says that the basis of prayer, like a fruit from which everything comes, is to reach an inner peace, a total abandonment to God. It is from this peace that divine gifts derive. But if you are agitated then you cannot understand the will of God. Several times She has said:

> Every agitation comes from Satan.

How to Reach Depth in Prayer

Lastly, I want to tell you to set out on the pilgrimage of the messages. During this time, I have understood that the entire spiritual life consists of deep prayer. To enter spiritual life in-depth means to enter prayer in-depth. Depth of prayer is reached by praying, fasting and loving. I have seen that Our Lady has stressed these three elements during this period. You must pray not only with your lips but with your heart. Fast, love your enemies, love those who are suffering, love your neighbours, love everyone. It is by these means that it is possible to reach depth in prayer and reach a spiritual life. I repeat once more: set out on the path of the messages and of prayer. Never say that you have no time for God; God is of no use to me; God cannot help me; I can live without God. All this means having no time for God. From my own experience I tell you to try to pray morning and evening. At least half an hour each morning and evening so that we can feel one with God. You will then see how the spiritual life within you reawakens and continually increases.

Words of Consolation

From Jelena

Now some words of consolation for you. You ask for graces and Our Lady says:

> You can receive as many as you wish, it depends on you: pray, pray, pray.

Our Lady once said:

> Do not be surprised because I often say: pray, pray, pray. I have nothing else to tell you.

I must mention something else. Our Lady said:

> When I tell you 'pray' do not understand this as meaning only an increase in the number of prayers: I want to bring you to an attitude of a continuous longing and desire for God.

Our life must be transformed into a day of prayer. Our Lady said: 'Pray when you can. Pray how you can, but always pray more and more.' And then added, 'Each of you could pray even for four hours a day. But I know that many people do not understand this because they think they can live by their work alone.'

I said: 'If I tell people this, they will turn away.'

She replied: 'Even you do not understand this. It is only a sixth of your day.'

I added: 'I understand that you want us to pray all day.' Then She seemed happy.

I tell you that it is really possible to pray all day, to be in contact with God all day long. When I told the people, they looked at me in a rather amazed way. I asked them what they did after half an hour's heavy work in the fields? They get up and try to rest for a while. So I asked them why not say 'Jesus help me'? Why not say then 'Jesus bless what I have done'? Why not keep in contact with God while you rest so that He may bless your work? This is how you can transform prayer into a continuous prayer. We must remember what Our Lady said in the Autumn:

> Do not forget: man does not live by work alone
> but also by prayer. Your work will not go well
> without prayer.

In fact, in the beginning of the planting season in Medjugorje I told the parishioners: 'If you want to tire yourselves out while planting the tobacco, do not pray and work very hard. But if you want God to help you plant the tobacco – which is very difficult here because the earth is dry, water has to be carried and the plants protected – if you want God to work for you and for you to rest then come to church.' They came to church more frequently and everything went easily. They did not even have to carry one drop of water for the tobacco. God sent rain at the right moment.

I am giving you this example, so that you can understand that we really must pray more; if we do not pray more, we are not truly converted.

One more point I want to stress is this: if we want to be honest with God, we must recognise that we have put Him away in a corner. The worst sin in your families is that television has become like a god in your homes. Television dictates the routine in your homes, the timetable, how to behave, how to use your time. And God has no rights in your families. He remains in a corner. If you understand Our Lady properly then put God in the centre and the television in the corner. The television can only be watched when God allows it and not the other way around. We must reverse our values. You must bring order in your homes if you want to pray. If the television is at the centre of your day, there is no room for God there. If many objects and gadgets in your homes are the centre, God cannot be there. Make your home simple and you will see how close God is to you.

I will give you another piece of advice. Our Lady said:

> I should be very happy if families would pray
> for half an hour each morning and evening.

Many people were amazed when they learned this, but really each family should do this if it wants to progress spiritually. If you want to live each day with God you need at least twenty minutes prayer each morning. You will then be in a condition to spend the day with God. Those who say that the whole of their day belongs to God are not telling the truth if they do not pray enough. When you spend a day like this, in the evening you will need about half an hour to unload yourself of all the difficulties you have collected during the day and to be in peace.

It is really very little if we look at the divine promises, at what God is offering us. I am telling you this in order to explain a way of growth in your spiritual lives. If people only pray a little in the morning and then make the sign of the cross and just do the same in the evening, they cannot progress spiritually, they will become more and more restless and distracted. They want graces granted quickly, they want to push a button. They think: to be healthy, I must sleep seven or eight hours. How can we live with God within us if we do not dedicate any time for this? It is impossible. All work takes a certain time. We must dedicate some silent, serious time to God. People usually say that they have no time. I can assure you that this is most untrue because I have seen many of these people who say they have no time, but watch television until midnight. When there is a football match everybody gets up and runs.

I will tell you something else: if you use your time for God, God will use time for you, for your children and many problems will disappear. If you pray you will not come here to ask for graces to be granted because they will be granted in your homes. If you reduce your prayers to a minimum, then you will receive a minimum: it will be given to you according to your measure. Our Lady has recommended various means of praying, emphasising prayer, fasting, not being worried, but allowing God to act. Learn this rule. Watch people when they enter church: they are worn out, full of fear and this is not a good thing. We have not abandoned ourselves to God; our belongings and difficulties are more important to us than He is. Especially of late, people have been running up to me to say that their daughter is ill, she has this or that, for example, but almost no one has said to me that they have a problem: they have not been converted. This is a reversal of values and graces cannot be granted in such superficiality of soul. First of all we must be converted. This is why Our Lady tells us, first of all, to read the passage in the Gospel of St Matthew 6:24–34: 'Make it your first care to find the Kingdom of God.'

That is my conversion. Then you can ask for graces to be granted. If there is the right attitude within me, right according to the Gospel, I shall not worry. When I am not worried about these things my soul is free and God can act in it. If I am full of fears, of worries, I am closed to God. Remember that Our Lady said:

> Pray, fast and allow God to act.

Our Lady has given us another rule:

> If you want to be very happy, live a simple, humble life, pray a great deal and do not delve into your problems, let God resolve them.

Another rule that you must learn is to simplify your homes, because life has become complicated: all those clothes, toys and pleasures. Give all this to the poor and you will be free and less worried. When you have problems, do not have them analysed or go here and there trying to find out what has happened: leave them to God. You must pray and have faith.

Here is another rule. Our Lady said:

> Peace must follow your prayer.

The beginning, during, and at the end of prayer must be followed by peace. About prayer and especially group prayers, Our Lady says:

> Often prayers recited aloud in a loud voice sends Jesus away because men want to win through their efforts. In that way there is no place for God. Prayers recited aloud are good but they must come from peace and from the heart.

Our Lady then said:

> Even the joy, the singing can be an obstacle in
> the groups if people are only moving emo-
> tionally.

All the messages of Our Lady can be summed up in one
word: *Pray*. When I tell you to pray I have not said enough.
By listening to the daily messages of Our Lady, I
understood that when we pray sufficiently we acquire a
desire for God, a continuous contact with God. I remember
another message given by Our Lady:

> When I tell you to pray, pray, pray you must not
> understand just an increase in the number of
> prayers. I want to bring you to a deep desire for
> God. That you may always desire God.

I understood then that to have a continuous desire for
God means to pray. I remembered what Our Lady once
said, on Holy Thursday, I believe, in answer to my question:
'Dear Mother, can you tell us how Jesus was able to pray
for one whole day and night? What method did He use?'
She replied: 'He had a great desire for God and the
salvation of souls.' I then remembered that prayer comes
from a great desire for God and for the salvation of souls. If
you put yourself before God with this attitude of Our Lady
you will realise the things that need changing in your
family life and in your private life in order to acquire this
desire for God.

Meditating on this, I discovered that we Christians are
like sick people because we have lost our appetite for God.
We have an appetite for eating and sleeping but people
have to make an effort to pray. Prayer has become an effort
because the desire for God is lacking and He is not at the

centre of our lives. In order to effect the conversion Our Lady speaks of, we must progress so as to reach a prayer which is a desire for God.

I explained to the parishioners how they could pray continuously. I told them that when they went into the fields, to pray as they went. After an hour's work and they are tired, to get up and rest a while and to say: Jesus, I want to rest in You; Jesus, bless what I have done. This really is a continuous prayer, a breath of God. Try to find contact with God all the time. Seek His blessing and give Him everything.

Our Lady wishes to bring about this attitude in us. It seems to me that, with this attitude to prayer, we will reach the point in which God will be the centre of our families and our homes. It is my conviction that to put God at the centre of our lives is to put prayer at the centre of our lives, to desire God continuously and to discover the deepest values of Christianity.

It is through prayer that we realise this meeting with God.

From Fr Tomislav

During this month, the last one of three years of apparitions (which began on 24th–25th June 1981), Our Lady has repeatedly said: 'Pray, pray, pray.' We cannot understand the message without prayer; spoken and written words are empty without prayer, without an inner attitude; it is only through this inner attitude to pray that light comes to us, by which we can really feel what God wants at this moment.

From the beginning of the apparitions Our Lady has constantly said:

Christians who do not pray at all are no longer Christians; those who pray a little are only a little Christian and those who pray enough, well, are good Christians.

In order, therefore, to live prayer and to truly deepen it we need to look at certain elements which can help us. After meditating on what Our Lady had said during this period, I understood that She wants us to pray twenty-four hours a day. Our Lady is right when She tells us to stop watching television. Television has become like a god in your homes, deciding how families spend their free time. This is the god you adore. If you want to understand prayer, put the television set in a corner and put God in the centre of your homes. It is God who must put order in your family and who must decide your routine.

I have given you this picture to explain how many of the things in your families, in your worries have become your god, and I have discovered a real and serious sickness amongst Christians: we need to eat and when we lose our appetites we think we are ill; we need to sleep and if someone cannot sleep we say that person is ill; Christians who do not feel a need to pray and just make an effort to do so are sick and when Our Lady says that She wants us to pray more She brings us exactly to this.

Once Our Lady told Jelena:

When I tell you to pray, pray, pray you must not understand just an increase in the number of prayers. I want to bring you to a deep desire for God. That you may always desire God.

Here I have discovered what Our Lady wishes: that, by means of prayer, of seeking God, we reach an attitude of a continuous desire for God. Here is an example: two people in love with each other think of each other all the time, write letters, dream: they are always united. When there is true faith in us, we are united to God. I need to be there; I am tired without God; I need to rest in prayer; I have many serious problems; I need to go to God and tell Him what is happening to me; when I am full of joy I go to God to share my joy with Him. This is the attitude to which Our Lady wants to bring all of us, but, instead, we pray in fragments – I pray for five minutes and that time is dedicated to God but the rest of the time is for my material welfare. Whilst our prayers are so partitioned, we cannot reach real Christianity, we cannot reach a real life with God.

Jesus had a great desire for God; I think we can only reach this attitude to prayer if we reawaken this desire for God, we need to start to search for Him, to rediscover Him. In this age, we have really thrown God into a corner, preferring machines, science and everything else and we have forgotten God. Now we must rediscover Him, live Him and we can do this only through prayer. Often people ask me how they can pray, how they can find peace in prayer. This is my answer, if you accept it. It is simple: you have the rosary, you have the Gospel. Your priests will tell you everything else in church. The rosary and the Gospel. It is only necessary to dedicate enough time to God. Put order in your families but see that there is time for God in your daily routine; make a note of it, make a programme: this is time for God in my family, and do not let anyone take it away from you. Then ask Jesus to be the guide of your family and do not worry about your problems. Start to talk to God, to read the Gospel and to pray. Soon you will discover how that inner peace comes, in a happiness which comes from God, because we really found Him, because we have spoken to Him.

What is happening in Medjugorje is a tangible fact. Each of us can find different interpretations of the apparitions. It is only possible to make suppositions. As far as we priests who live here are concerned everything is very clear. I, personally, have seen that all these events have led me forward towards God and towards my fellow beings. As I feel truly helped along this path, then it must be real. During this period here, I have discovered Our Lady in a new light and I have come to realise that we have not yet discovered Her strength. Most people, also priests, regard Her as one of the saints. It is my opinion that we are about to enter into a new era when we will discover Our Lady in Her full light and understand Her special role.

After the Second Vatican Council, we have seen many groups and movements springing up and I see the apparitions of Our Lady as purification of all this spiritual growth. I put a precise question to Our Lady: 'Have you come to purify these movements?' She replied: 'It is exactly so.'

I see Our Lady here as an event and as a person who will take us beyond all movements, because in all these movements there exists our individual manner of organisation, our human subjectivity. Our Lady is above all this and what has impressed me, is that Christian prayer must be above all methodology.

She has often repeated:

> Prayer is a dialogue with God. It is a discovery
> of the Gospel.

Here it is not a question of any special method of concentration in prayer or methodology, although we can each have our own method. It is something natural, just as a sick person has his own way of praying, so a young person has another way and so on. But I have seen that the prayer Our Lady speaks of brings us to discover Jesus. When we asked what Our Lady thought of oriental meditation, She replied:

> Why do you call it meditation, when it is human work? True meditation is a meeting with Jesus when you will discover joy and inner peace.

She is really saying: to be very happy, be united to God. We can see that everything is centred on a personal meeting with God and this is the context of the pilgrimage which Our Lady is making with us. The path of prayer is, at the same time, a path of faith to discover Jesus Christ. Once Our Lady said:

> You must know that there is only one God and only one Meditator, Jesus Christ.

It seems to me that this pilgrimage Our Lady is making with us is a pilgrimage of faith and prayer for a personal meeting with God through which the meaning of many movements is clarified. I have found this problem, that many people, even priests, look to the visionaries and Our Lady for rules, formula, but there are none. We have to go beyond these. I will explain: during all this time, Our Lady has never given a formula to anyone, but has only given us brief words: 'Pray, pray, pray' and 'Be converted'. These are more of a stimulus, not a theology, not a treatise, but an inducement to open our hearts. Priests must take a step forward, beyond those words and discover, by the light of the Holy Spirit, the whole content of the words. When I am in my parish I must have the light within so as to bring that content to people, because words without content are empty. This is the reason why Our Lady has said several times:

> Pray to the Holy Spirit that He may descend upon you. People pray in the wrong way; they go to shrines, to churches, to ask for special graces, but few are those who ask for the Holy Spirit. Those who receive the Holy Spirit have already received everything.

She often advises us to pray for the gift of the Holy Spirit so that we may be enlightened. I see this as being extremely important for priests, so that we may have inner light to conduct ourselves by this light, to understand the subject matter. We will be able in this way to lead people onwards. We have seen here that people want to be saved easily: press a button and expect special graces at once. Here, by divine providence, we have been able to save the shrine, save the apparitions. I am sure that the apparitions were saved because people came into the church. The police had forbidden people to go on the mountainside, and in this way we have been in a position to guide them. Otherwise, people transform everything into superstition, into something superficial.

Those who have studied these things have told me about what has happened in several shrines where Our Lady has appeared. The priests withdrew and the visionaries were left alone and were turned into something like automatic machines for everything and that the nucleus of the apparitions has been literally covered with money and superficial objects.

We discovered the case of a lay person who had been bringing people here, giving them his own explanations.

These were terrible: how women should be dressed; how the Holy Eucharist should be received; how a woman who has had an abortion cannot be pardoned and goes to Hell; and all this attributed to Our Lady! Words that have never been spoken by Our Lady Here! We can see that where there is no guidance from the Church people will say anything, they bring their fanaticism, their problems, and leave them here. I see that it is most important for priests to feel the responsibility for guiding people. Our Lady is appearing in order to reawaken us and we must go forward, understand and remember the words, just as Our Lady remembered the words spoken about Jesus. I feel this as being important.

Another thing I consider important and something that I would encourage priests in parishes to do is to call everyone to a minimum of prayer and fasting. I have discovered that the greatest sin of the Christian today is indifference. A majority of the faithful are in practice unfaithful. They do not pray, they do not fast, they do not practice anything, they are carried away by society and behave like everybody else. If we succeed in bringing them to at least a minimum of spiritual activity they will come out from their indifference. Our Lady has a very good lesson for us when, at the beginning of the apparition she said:

> Say every day at least seven Our Fathers, Hail
> Marys, Glory Bes, and the Creed and begin to
> fast every Friday.

In my opinion this is not enough for a Christian. It means we are below a minimum of at least seven minutes direct relationship with Jesus. If we succeed in bringing people to a minimum of prayer, fasting, renunciation, then at home, in the family, something will start moving and people will lose their indifference. Then some generous people from the parish will come forward, who will go ahead and you will be able to form various active groups and start working together. In this way you will make the rest of the parish grow.

I think that this way of working is very important in order to unite the whole parish and to allow spontaneous prayer groups and renewal groups to come out of their ghettos. Yes, I have seen many groups close in on themselves, but not others. I see that all groups can be corrected from within the parish and the parish priest can guide them together with the rest of the parish.

Be open towards all groups because they will be able to help the parish and at the same time, be corrected if you are open towards them. In all groups, I have seen some good initiatives but, if they are not helped and guided, they do not blossom. Later the group becomes like a small sect; this diminishes its strength and at the same time, creates problems in the parish. I think it most important that parish priests should be open towards all groups, because the groups are a human way of expression which can be improved and opened up when we are able to guide them. I have often seen that lay people have the spirit and the zeal but not the perspective that a priest should have in order to enlighten a movement and help it. I feel this is very important.

Everything undertaken with Our Lady receives more strength and the path with Her is easier. I have never found any difficulties in the group here that are not to be found in several other groups: certain fanaticisms, quarrels and jealousies. There is simplicity, harmony and peace, and simplicity is what Our Lady says about the path of faith. A total abandonment to God. I always say to the people who come here and ask me how they can pray that they have two things to take: the rosary and the Gospel, and that their priest will give them everything else. Start praying with simplicity. All the methods we know can help us, but we must not be worried about them, it is enough to set people out on the path of faith, before God.

On Holy Thursday 1984 She said:

> I will reveal a spiritual secret to you: if you want to be stronger than evil, make yourselves an active conscience, that is, pray sufficiently in the morning, read a passage from the Gospel and root the Divine Word in your hearts and live it during the day, particularly in your trials, in this way you will become stronger all the time.

I heard about having an active conscience for the first time in my life from a girl of eleven, Jelena, who brought Our Lady's message. I can see that through this active conscience we enter into a permanent and continuous prayer and only in this way can we grow. Otherwise I realise that our prayers leave us in a closed circle: I pray but remain as before; I go to confession but remain as before; this active conscience takes me forward all the time and all the points given to us by Our Lady – that is interior prayer for at least half an hour every morning and evening, strengthen this active conscience. I will explain: if a person who is mentally sick does not take medicine, tranquillisers, he will get worse because he will have frightening dreams and in the morning will get up feeling tired. During the day he will continue to accumulate difficulties and his sleep will deteriorate. The tension increases so the doctors prescribe medicines to halt this. So it is with us, in prayer, if we pray each morning, if we can be cleansed and purified in our hearts and abandon ourselves completely to God, we can live the day. In the evening, we must be unloaded of all our burdens in order to sleep during the night with a light heart; in the morning we will feel better. In this way we make progress all the time.

Once Our Lady said to little Jelena:

> Your days will be different according to whether you pray in the evening or not.

If we have a continuous rhythm for a direct relationship with God, our inner strength will increase, the light will increase and we will always be on the way forward.

Question: Is there anything special for priests to stress?
Our Lady has not said anything in particular for priests. When we asked for advice, She said at the beginning:

> Be strong in your faith and protect the faith of your people.

Once I asked what She recommended for Advent and She replied: 'Do what the Church tells you.' Another time I asked if She wanted to give a sign to priests so that they may believe and She said:

> Let them take the Gospel. Let them believe and they will understand everything.

The answers are for a reawakening, as they are for all the faithful.

Question: With regard to the consecration of the world to the Immaculate Heart of Mary that the Pope made on 25 March 1984, according to the directions of Fatima, has Our Lady given any practical guidance on how to carry it out and make it vivid and alive?

I cannot give you a precise reply to this as Our Lady has not referred to it directly, but last year we prepared for a long time for the Consecration of the Parish. In November 1983 Our Lady expressly said it was Her desire that all families consecrate themselves every day to the Heart of Jesus and the Immaculate Heart. So, before Christmas, we started a preparation of forty days; until the Feast Day of the Immaculate Conception everybody went to confession and every evening we took the path of purification. We then went towards Christmas trying to live the Word in our purified hearts. During this period Our Lady always encouraged us: 'Concentrate on the heart, words are not enough, concentrate on the heart.' You see I am giving you the answer to what Our Lady wants; She wants to inspire our hearts not our tongues. To live the faith with our hearts. I think that is the only purpose of the Consecration: that is, to get closer to the heart of Jesus with the help of the Immaculate Heart of Mary.

The last three messages I will speak of are typical: at one time, Our Lady said:

> Dear children, at this time Satan wants to obstruct all my plans. Pray so that he will not succeed. I will pray to my Son so that you may feel His victory.

Soon after, She said:

> You have felt the presence of Satan during this
> week: Do not be worried. God is watching over
> all of you. I have given myself for you and I
> participate in each of your trials. Do not be
> afraid.

And soon after that there was a strong appeal to increase
prayer, especially by young people, to increase prayer and
sacrifice. Our Lady repeated this many times, both to the
young people and the parish and to those who were
present.

Ivan tells us that Our Lady has promised to give special
grace to people who pray, fast and open their hearts during
this time. Now She has asked for a heartfelt confession and
a true participation in the Holy Eucharist.

The entire spiritual life Our Lady speaks of consists in
the deepening of prayer. We can see clearly that we must
deepen our prayer if we want to see our spiritual life
deepen. It is a parallelism: to deepen our prayer is to
deepen our spiritual life. Those who have abandoned
themselves to God in their spiritual life have no difficulty
to pray: prayer is sweet to them.

We learn to pray by praying, fasting and loving. These
are the three elements we can see on this path. Another very
important issue is this: many Christians behave like
atheists. From the beginning we have seen people coming
here who did not pray at all or hardly at all.

Everyone complained: 'We can recite seven Our Fathers,
Hail Marys, Glory Bes, but is it compulsory?' We have seen
that the Christian mentality is like this: to put God in the
last place in our daily lives. When we speak of seven Our
Fathers, Hail Marys, Glory Bes, there are Christians who

say, 'I have no time, I have to work, I cannot manage it …'
But truly, when I stand before God as now and say 'I have
no time to say seven Our Fathers, Hail Marys, Glory Bes' I
feel ashamed. How can I be one of the faithful of Almighty
God, of God who is everything to me, and not have time
for Him? I am truly ashamed. When people say they have
no time to pray I always tell them they have twenty-four
hours a day, but they use this time for pleasant things.
When we do not have time for God it means that we do not
like Him; He comes last in our life. We have not discovered
Him.

I will explain: prayer means searching for God.

The Gospel tells us that the most important Com-
mandment is to love God with all our strength, with all our
being and to love our neighbours as ourselves. How do two
people behave when they are in love? They seek each other
all day, they dream of each other because they love each
other with all their heart. Time does not exist for them: I
love you for five minutes, I look for you for five minutes; it
cannot exist. If we look at our Christianity, if we are
searching for God, it cannot be for five minutes, or two
minutes. This cannot be. This is not true Christianity; true
Christianity is to love God with all our strength, to be in
love with Him.

I have discovered a serious problem: we Christians have
lost the need to pray. Man has certain needs: the need to eat,
the need to sleep; when I do not eat I feel hungry, when I
do not pray … I feel nothing! A great many Christians feel
nothing when they pray. They do not feel the need to. This
illness is like a form of atheism. I have realised this now
because I cannot live without God.

'Maran-Atha'
'Come Lord Jesus'

About the Editor

Finbar O'Leary first went to Medjugorje in May 1986. While in church on his first evening at 6.40 p.m., the time of Our Lady's apparition, he underwent an extraordinary spiritual experience. Touched by Our Lady, he wished his whole life to change; it did.

Shortly after returning home he suffered a stroke. Early one morning in hospital a holy priest with a wonderful gift of healing came into his room by mistake. He prayed over Finbar, who was instantly restored to full health.

Finbar tells how it took him at least six months to fully understand the great miracle that had occurred. Directed by this good priest, a three-year journey commenced seeking a clearer understanding and love for God the Father, Son and Holy Spirit, and of course Our Lady.

On his third visit to Medjugorje, now leading a group of one hundred and eighty pilgrims including seven priests, he met and was prayed over by the renowned Sr Briege McKenna who foretold for him that a great cross would come into his life and from this cross a most beautiful crown would be made for Our Lady. Over the years Sr Briege has prayed often with Finbar and seen the road that he must travel, Jesus walking at his side with His arm around him.

Having consecrated his life to Our Lady and Jesus, Finbar now travels extensively to spread the messages of

Medjugorje, to encourage the formation of prayer groups, and, having received the Charismatic Gift of Healing in 1989, to pray with people for healing.

Finbar was invited to return to Macedonia to give a Lenten retreat in the only Roman Catholic church in that country, after which he was told by many of the hundreds of Orthodox and Muslims who travelled great distances to attend that he was the only Catholic who had ever offered to pray with them.

His first book *Prayers and Hymns for Prayer Groups* is a most useful guide for both existing prayer groups and for individuals intending to form new prayer groups.

You may also enjoy ...

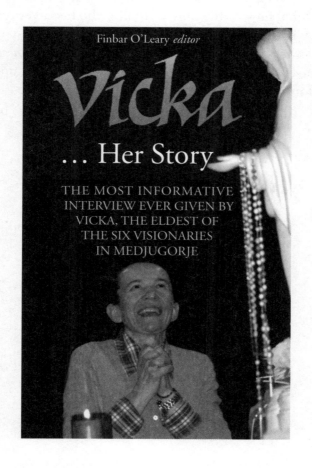

Finbar O'Leary *editor*

Vicka

... Her Story

THE MOST INFORMATIVE
INTERVIEW EVER GIVEN BY
VICKA, THE ELDEST OF
THE SIX VISIONARIES
IN MEDJUGORJE